# FIVE MILLION STEPS

www.amplifypublishinggroup.com

*Five Million Steps: Hiking the Pacific Crest Trail after Three Decades of Service to Our Nation*

©2024 Jason France. All Rights Reserved. No part of this publication may be reproduced, stored in a retrieval system or transmitted in any form by any means electronic, mechanical, or photocopying, recording or otherwise without the permission of the author.

There are chapters in this book that discuss themes of child neglect, bullying, combat-related trauma, post-traumatic stress and anxiety, substance abuse, and addiction that can be triggering for some readers. Please proceed with caution if these topics are sensitive to you. If you are in crisis, please contact the 988 Suicide & Crisis Lifeline. Call or text 988, or go to 988lifeline.org/chat to access live chat. You will be connected with a trained crisis counselor who will listen to you, provide support, and get you the help you need. The author and Amplify Publishing Group assume no liability for accidents happening to, or injuries sustained by, readers who engage in activities described in this book. The author has tried to recreate events, locales, and conversations from his memories of them. In order to maintain anonymity in some instances, the author has changed the names of individuals and places, and may have changed some identifying characteristics and details.

For more information, please contact:
Amplify Publishing, an imprint of Amplify Publishing Group
620 Herndon Parkway, Suite 220
Herndon, VA 20170
info@amplifypublishing.com

Library of Congress Control Number: 2024903749
CPSIA Code: PRV0524A
HARDCOVER ISBN: 979-8-89138-235-0
PAPERBACK ISBN: 979-8-89138-236-7
Printed in the United States

*To Monica, Joseph, and Justin.*
*You are my heart.*
*You are my world.*
*I love you.*

JASON FRANCE

# FIVE MILLION STEPS

*Hiking the Pacific Crest Trail after Three Decades of Service to Our Nation*

# CONTENTS

Chapter 1: My First Steps ........................................1

Chapter 2: Identity ..................................................9

Chapter 3: Hike Your Own Hike ............................19

Chapter 4: Seen through a Different Lens..................27

Chapter 5: Disconnecting......................................39

Chapter 6: Gratitude............................................45

Chapter 7: Connection.........................................55

Chapter 8: Badass Dad.........................................73

Chapter 9: In the Moment.....................................89

Chapter 10: Simplicity .........................................99

Chapter 11: Into the Darkness .............................105

Chapter 12: The Path to Healing..........................125

Chapter 13: Overcoming the Obstacles..................135

Chapter 14: Putting Myself First ..........................157

Chapter 15: Evolution.........................................163

Chapter 16: Success ...........................................175

Chapter 17: After the Trail...................................197

ABOUT THE AUTHOR.......................................205

CHAPTER 1

# MY FIRST STEPS

*There it is! This is really happening!* I thought as the Toyota Prius rounded the last curve on the bumpy gravel road that led to the trail's starting point.

In front of me stood the monument at the southern terminus of the Pacific Crest Trail (PCT). I had dreamed about this moment for over forty years, since I was a child. Seeing the monument for the first time gave me a rush of excitement and nervousness as I wondered what I would experience over the coming months.

It was six thirty in the morning on Sunday, April 18, 2021, and I was about to start what would turn out to be the most amazing adventure of my life: hiking 2,650 miles from the border of Mexico to the border of Canada, through California, Oregon, and Washington. It's been said it takes over five million steps to complete the PCT. It passes through seven national parks and twenty-five national forests, crosses over one hundred major mountain passes, and has over four hundred thousand feet of elevation gain along the trail.

The weeks leading up to starting my PCT journey had been a blur. I retired from the United States Air Force on the first of April, after serving our nation for over thirty-one years. The hike was more than making one of my childhood dreams come true. It was also to celebrate my retirement as well as my fiftieth birthday, which I celebrated only a week before starting.

I had arrived in San Diego on the fourteenth, partly to acclimate for a few days in the dry climate and heat—much different from what I'd left in Illinois—but also to get my mind focused on what my life would look like for the next five months. As I landed at San Diego International Airport, I saw hundreds of young marines training at Marine Corps Recruit Depot, San Diego. The airport runway is parallel to the base. They were just starting their journeys in the military, while I had just ended mine and was about to start my next big journey.

Seeing them made me wonder about all the amazing things they would see and do during their time in the military, how serving our nation would impact their lives, the bonds they would build with their fellow marines, the challenges they would overcome, the successes they would enjoy together, the places they'd go, and the differences they would make in the lives of people around the world. Although my journey would be completely different from the journey these young marines were starting, seeing them also made me wonder what I would see and experience on the PCT. What challenges would I face? What bonds would I build with the people I shared the experience with? How would the journey change me?

I stayed at an Airbnb in a quiet part of the city to relax and prepare with no distractions. My days were filled with shopping for the final few items I needed, taking long walks around the city to get used to the temperature, staying hydrated, working on my flexibility, and doing as much research as I could on the weather and trail conditions while I still had internet access.

The morning I started my journey, I dropped off my rental car at the airport and met with another hiker who was starting the same day. We were both members of an online PCT group, and when we learned we were starting the same day, we decided to share the ninety-minute taxi ride from the airport to the terminus outside the town of Campo. It was nice to talk with another hiker starting on the same day, also solo, and learn we both had similar excitement, concerns, and thoughts about what we would soon experience. We were both awestruck once the taxi dropped us off and we were standing at the monument.

The monument is constructed from five square wooden posts of various lengths, about twelve-by-twelve inches each. The shortest post is about knee high and the tallest about eight feet. The posts are all painted gray with thin black bands circling the top of each post. Three of the posts are engraved with black lettering: "SOUTHERN TERMINUS, PACIFIC CREST NATIONAL SCENIC TRAIL, ESTABLISHED BY ACT OF CONGRESS ON OCT 2, 1968," "MEXICO TO CANADA 2,650 MILES, 1988 A.D.," and "ELEVATION 2,915 FT." The PCT's emblem is displayed on the tallest post.

On the side of the monument is a small black metal box labeled "PCT Sign-In" that contains a notebook and pen inside a clear plastic bag. It was the first of many trail registers I would sign. They were dispersed along the trail, many in remote areas or at the beginning of difficult stretches. Not only was it a great way to see who was hiking ahead of you, but it was also helpful if a search party had to locate an injured or missing hiker.

Nearly everyone who starts at the southern terminus signs the register. I read a few pages and saw the names of hikers who began before me, the date they started, and where they were from. Many shared words of inspiration, meaningful quotes, or funny sayings, but I was so nervous and excited that I couldn't think of anything clever. My hands were trembling as I simply wrote "4/18—Jay France—Mascoutah, IL."

The monument sat about twenty-five yards away from the partially constructed border wall that divides the United States and Mexico. The four-strand barbed-wire fence that used to mark the border was still standing too, only a few feet away from the monument. A common practice for hikers is to extend their foot or hand through the border wall into the Mexican side of the border so they can say they actually started in Mexico.

There were signs posted along the new wall that stated, "WARNING. THIS AREA PATROLLED BY U.S. BORDER PATROL. REMAIN 100′ FROM FENCE."

Despite the warning signs, I wanted to follow tradition. Standing near the barbed-wire fence, I looked around for any agents on patrol. There were none. The wall was still being constructed, and all I saw were construction vehicles and workers in both directions, but none close enough to concern me. After confirming the area was clear of anyone who could see me, I carefully climbed over the barbed-wire fence, ran across the gravel road that parallels the wall, and stuck my hand between the steel slats and into Mexico, making my start point official.

Rushing across the road again and climbing back over the fence, I saw a border patrol agent in the distance, fast approaching on an all-terrain vehicle, a trail of dust kicking up behind him. He was on the gravel road we'd used to get to the terminus. The buzzing of his ATV got louder as he approached, coming directly toward me. *Great. I'm going to get rolled up before I even start.*

I thought he was alone when I first spotted him and saw what seemed to be a large pack on his back. When he got close enough for me to see him clearly, I realized there was a small person on the back of his ATV. *Does he have a kid with him? No, that's a hiker. Is this dude out here detaining hikers wandering too close to the border?* A small hand waved at me as they pulled up. It turned out the hiker had been making her way on foot to the terminus from a nearby camp when the border patrol agent picked her up. The agent gave us some information about the area and wished us all good luck before speeding off. I hadn't even started hiking yet, and I'd already had the first three of what would become countless memorable experiences with people I encountered on the trail.

After a few final photos at the monument, I took my first steps on the PCT. The sound of the rocky ground crunching under my feet is still sharp in my mind. I also remember the "Phew!" I let out, loud enough to hear over the crunch of my footsteps, and the feeling of relief from finally being on the trail after months of planning and preparation and years of dreaming about it. I was hit with more excitement and nerves, and flooded with thoughts as I continued. *Am I ready for this? Can I make it all the way to Canada? Only time will tell. Just take it one day at a time.*

The PCT is comprised of five sections. The first is the southern California section, commonly known as the desert section, and runs seven hundred miles from the Mexican border, near Campo, to the community of Kennedy Meadows. The desert section passes through the Mojave Desert and five mountain ranges. The section is often noted for its extreme temperature variations, windy conditions, and limited water sources, but it also offers incredible vistas and some of the most amazing sunrises and sunsets I have ever viewed.

Next is the central California section, or mountain section, which runs over four hundred miles through the Sierra Nevada mountain range before ending near Donner Pass. The mountain section is most noted for its stunning scenery, high elevation, tough climbs and descents, snowfield traverses, and sometimes challenging river and stream crossings as it winds through towering granite peaks, glacially carved canyons, and pristine alpine lakes. In this section, the trail passes through Sequoia, Kings Canyon, and Yosemite national parks. Additionally, the trail crosses eight named mountain passes above eleven thousand feet in elevation, the most notable of which is Forester Pass, the highest point on the PCT, at 13,200 feet.

Third is the northern California section. It runs the 540 miles from Donner Pass to the border of California and Oregon. Continuing through the Sierra Nevada mountain range, the trail gradually transitions into lower elevations as it enters the southern Cascade Range and passes through Lassen Volcanic National Park. This section is often the most mentally challenging for hikers, as the spectacular views of the Sierra Nevada are gone, the temperatures are typically the highest of the trail, and the reality of the length of the trail through California sets in.

The Oregon section is a welcome change after hiking almost 1,700 miles through California. It's 455 miles long and is the flattest section of the PCT. Its lower elevation, dense forests, and less rugged terrain mean high-mileage days for most while still providing views of the volcanic peaks that make up the Cascade Range. Additionally, the trail passes through Crater Lake National Park. At the border of Oregon and Washington, the Columbia River Gorge is the lowest point on the trail, at 180 feet in elevation.

Finally, the Washington section, the last 505 miles of the trail, brings hikers back into rugged and scenic mountainous terrain and is said by many to be the most beautiful, but also the most physically demanding, section of the PCT. Washington's unpredictable and sometimes severe weather often poses challenges, as autumn is approaching when most northbound hikers are in this section. The trail passes near Mount Adams, goes through Goat Rocks Wilderness, passes Mount Rainier, and enters Glacier Peak Wilderness before moving into Lake Chelan National Recreation Area. It finishes in North Cascades National Park at the border of Washington and Canada.

• • •

It took about an hour of hiking for my mind to calm down and start taking in all the sights, sounds, and smells of my new surroundings: the beautiful but rugged landscape of the southern California desert, the whoosh of wind rushing through the trees, and the fragrant green grasses and manzanita trees. The trail, and all that came with it, would be home for the next five months. I was doing something not many people ever get to do: fulfilling a true childhood dream.

I was eight years old when I first learned about the PCT. I was at my grandmother's house, sitting in her living room, going through her collection of *National Geographic* magazines. The June 1971 issue was on the top of the stack I'd taken. The feature story was "Mexico to Canada on the Pacific Crest Trail." The cover illustration showed two hikers in Glacier Peak Wilderness in Washington and had a graphic representation of California, Oregon, and Washington, with a yellow line representing the trail. The thirty-eight-page article was packed with incredible photos that were the first thing that caught my attention. Goat Rocks, Glacier Peak, Crater Lake, and Mount Rainier; hikers with enormous packs and even bigger smiles; flowers, snow, and animals; and firefighters battling blazes. There were maps of each section too, and its scale blew me away. A mile seemed like a lot to me at that age—twenty-four hundred miles (the length of the PCT at the time of the article) seemed impossible.

My grandmother sat with me, and we read the article together. She was a great storyteller, and the excitement in her voice and expressions on her face got me excited too. The article also told the story of the first person to hike the entire trail. He hiked southbound and finished in 129 days. My grandmother told me I could hike it too, and probably faster than him. On that day, she planted the seed that grew into my dream of one day hiking the PCT.

Not only did she inspire me to hike the PCT, but she also fueled my passion for the outdoors. I was born and raised on Whidbey Island, Washington. Even as a kid, I knew I lived in a special place. My grandmother took me on walks on the beaches around the island. Our favorites were Libbey Beach Park, Fort Ebey State Park, and Fort Casey State Park. We went on clear days, when it was raining, and when it was foggy, whether the temperatures were warm or cold. We would explore for hours, hiking the trails near the beaches, searching for seashells, beach glass, agates, and driftwood. We'd watch the crabs, anemones, sea urchins, and starfish in the tide pools and investigate the interesting things that washed up on the beach.

We found something new every time we went on our adventures together. From the beaches we could see the snowcapped Olympic Mountains in Olympic National Park to the southwest. They were the first mountains I ever saw, and I remember being eager to explore them on my own someday.

My grandmother was building my sense of curiosity, appreciation and respect for nature, and desire to explore. The outdoors became the place I would go to escape, feel safe, and find peace and answers. She showed me the power nature has to heal. It became my church, my spirituality. What my grandmother gave me were gifts, and those gifts are sacred to me.

Watching an amazing sunset on my first night on the PCT, I realized how fortunate I was to live out my childhood dream, and how I needed to cherish every moment and every step of my journey.

CHAPTER 2

# IDENTITY

I retired from the United States Air Force as a chief master sergeant, an E-9, the highest enlisted grade. Congress limits the number of active-duty airmen who can hold the rank of chief to only 1 percent of the enlisted population.

In 2012, less than a year after being promoted to chief, I was selected for a duty outside of my functional specialty: command chief master sergeant. Command chiefs are the senior enlisted leaders for large organizations from the wing to the major command levels. Wings perform specific missions to support the air force. There are airlift, fighter, special operations, and training wings, to name a few. The air force had 144 wings when I retired. Major commands are the major subdivisions of the air force and are organized by mission or geographic region overseas. There are nine major commands in the air force.

My first command chief position was at the 75th Air Base Wing at Hill Air Force Base, Utah. Less than four years and three assignments later, I was selected as the command chief of a major command, Air Force Materiel Command at Wright-Patterson Air Force Base, Ohio.

Command chiefs are sometimes given the opportunity to serve in joint leadership positions, working with men and women from all services, as command senior enlisted leaders. I was selected as the command senior enlisted leader for United States Transportation Command at Scott Air Force Base, Illinois, one of the eleven combatant commands within the US Department of Defense, and served there for the last two and a half years of my career. In that position, I was one of the most senior enlisted leaders in the military.

It was an honor to serve in those positions and to leverage my experiences, influence, and network of other leaders across the military to help others. I carried the same passion for people throughout my career, never defined my self-worth by the rank or positions I held, and certainly never let any of the positions go to my head, but slowly, as hard as I tried to prevent it from happening, I lost a lot of my personal identity.

I have always understood and agreed that the formality of senior leadership positions—the customs and courtesies, traditions, and protocol—are all essential parts of a hierarchical structure like the military. And I appreciated the trust, admiration, and respect I earned through my actions. The close connections I made and maintained with people throughout my career were the most personally fulfilling and valuable aspects of being in the air force. I was proud to be a part of my people's lives and proud they were a part of mine, but the further I went, the fewer people there were who actually knew *me* on a personal level.

I became only "chief" in the eyes of many of the people I served with, but there was so much more to me than my rank, title, or position. Jay France, the proud husband and father who had passions and interests outside of his military profession, wasn't as important anymore, even though those were the things that made me the chief I was.

I constantly spoke about the importance of family, self-care, and pursuing passions outside of work. However, I was rarely asked about how I was doing in those areas by anyone outside my small circle of friends or colleagues at the office. Most of the time when I was engaging with a crowd or even one-on-one, it was mostly about business, cutting short any talk of personal matters and getting straight to what I could provide them: help with a project, advocacy for an issue important to them, career advice, or to connect them with someone in my network. All of those were important to my role of caring for people, but the transactional nature of the relationships, despite my efforts to make personal connections, wore on me a lot.

A chance encounter with a young staff sergeant during a work trip to England helped me realize how much my personal identity had been lost. I went to the dining facility for breakfast on my second morning there. I had just sat at my table when the staff sergeant asked if he could join me. He had recognized me from the night before when I visited his organization. I remembered him too; he had given an excellent briefing on his team's mission and, most importantly, highlighted the personal and professional accomplishments of the youngest members of his team. I saw he was a great leader, had great connections with his people, and had earned their trust and admiration.

"I'd love to have breakfast with you. Please, have a seat," I replied.

In all honesty, I was expecting a conversation like so many I'd had before with young leaders like him, answering questions about getting promoted, what a person needs to do to make chief, how to deal with difficult supervisors, or similar issues. This conversation was different, though. After I asked, and he shared details about himself and his family, he turned it around and asked me similar questions in return: how I met my wife, what I felt after my first son was born, what book I was reading, and what I liked to do for fun. He didn't ask one question about work, careers, promotions, or anything military related. It was all about sharing the most important things to us outside of our roles as military leaders.

It was such a refreshing and heartwarming experience, not only to learn about him but also to have someone show interest in *me*, not just "the chief."

Five Million Steps    **11**

Walking back to my lodging room, I reflected on the conversation and couldn't remember the last time I'd had a talk like that with someone outside of my immediate circle.

I'm proud of my service. I loved being a chief. I loved the people I served with. But near the end of my career, I was ready to just be Jay.

The PCT was the first place I was able to do that. It gave me the anonymity I was looking for and the opportunity to be my authentic self again, with no expectations to act a certain way and no image to uphold. I was just another hiker among the others. We were all hiking on the same trail, enduring the same conditions, and carrying everything we needed in our packs. It didn't matter what jobs we had, how much money we made, what kind of cars we drove, or what social status we held in the "real world." On the trail, we were all equal. No one knew me as a chief, and those who learned I used to be one didn't care. It was exactly what I needed.

As far as identity on the trail, trail names are an important, and sometimes hilarious, part of trail culture. A person's trail name is typically given by other hikers and is usually a result of something embarrassing or funny they witnessed you do, while a small number of hikers choose their own trail names. Trail names are easier to remember than someone's real name, often because of the story about how they were earned. They are also useful in breaking the ice with new hikers you meet when you each get to tell the stories behind your trail names.

I knew about them before starting my PCT hike but had never earned one on the trails I had hiked previously. I wasn't concerned with getting one when I started, though. I was perfectly content with just being Jay. But as luck would have it, I earned my trail name on my second day on the trail. It was earned through pain and embarrassment and was a true testament to the saying, "You can't make this stuff up."

I wore long pants, a long-sleeved shirt, and a wide-brimmed hat to protect myself from the blistering sun and constant wind in the desert. The shirt I wore was extremely popular among hikers. It was made of lightweight but durable polyester, was breathable and comfortable, and dried quickly. I found one major issue with the shirt on the second day, though, an issue I hadn't realized when I wore it at home during training hikes before leaving. The shirt had two chest pockets lined with a mesh material designed to keep the shirt thin and breathable.

My first day on the trail, still not acclimated to the southern California heat, I sweated profusely over the eleven miles I covered. I didn't feel it when I was moving, but as soon as I stopped for the day, I noticed that both my nipples were stinging like crazy. When I took off my shirt, I saw they had been rubbed almost raw from the mesh material inside my chest pockets. I rinsed myself of the sweat and dust, put on a clean T-shirt, and soon the pain stopped. In my excitement of being in my first camp, having my first dinner on the trail, and watching my first sunset, I completely forgot about the chafing and went to sleep.

The next morning, I had an eight-and-a-half-mile hike to Lake Morena, where I planned to grab lunch and a milkshake at the Oak Shores Malt Shop, the first of many iconic PCT stops. Less than a mile out of camp, my nipples were stinging again, and I knew I would have problems if I didn't take care of the chafing soon. I decided to push on, though, waiting to take care of myself when I got to Lake Morena. That turned out to be a very poor decision.

About halfway to the lake, I met another hiker, a recently retired firefighter from San Francisco. The first twenty-two years of my career were spent in military law enforcement, and we bonded quickly. We both had strong type A personalities and found humor in jabbing at each other. He was a much faster hiker than me, and we hiked together for about thirty minutes before parting ways, knowing we'd see each other at the lake.

After we separated and I was alone again, I noticed my nipples hurt even more and that they were bleeding through my shirt. I still didn't stop and take care of myself, though. I was too sweaty for Band-Aids or athletic tape

Five Million Steps   **13**

to stay on. I wanted to get to the lake as quickly as possible and deal with everything there.

I arrived at Lake Morena right as the heat of the day kicked in. My shirt was soaked with sweat, and I had two pink spots on my chest where the blood had mixed with the sweat. I was not in the best of moods and didn't want any hikers who were likely gathered at the malt shop to know about my problem. I also didn't want anyone seeing the blood on my shirt or asking questions about what had happened. I wanted that milkshake and lunch, though, so I used the little water I had left to partially wash away the bloody spots from my shirt before heading to the malt shop.

Fortunately, only three other hikers were there, and none of them noticed anything. I ordered a fried-chicken sandwich and a mint chocolate chip milkshake, bought some Band-Aids and a tube of Neosporin, and waited for my food. I knew it would take a few days for my wounds to heal, and I didn't want to use any of the supplies I had in my small first aid kit.

After quickly eating my lunch, I took the short walk to Lake Morena County Park, where PCT hikers usually relax and wait out the heat of the day. There are picnic tables, restrooms, large trees providing shade, and a campground with pay showers. I planned to stay there for a few hours to cool off, clean myself up, and tend to my bleeding nipples before getting back on the trail.

My first order of business was to get clean. I went into the shower with everything on but my shoes. I needed to get the sweat, salt stains, dust, and blood off my clothes. I knew they would dry quickly in the heat and sun, even while wearing them. The cold water felt amazing, and I was surprised at all the dust and grime that washed down the drain after being on the trail for only a day and a half.

My clothes dried off within an hour as I napped on a picnic table under a huge oak tree. Then it was time to dress my wounds. I saw no one near the bathroom as I approached. Once inside, I yelled, "Hello? Is anyone in here?"

Nothing. *Nice, nobody needs to see this!*

I stood in front of a mirror and held my shirt open with one hand as I rubbed Neosporin on one of my nipples with the other. Just then, another hiker came around the corner and froze, eyes wide open, staring directly at me. I froze too, index finger still on my nipple. It was the firefighter.

"What the fuck, bro!" he said with a loud laugh. "What are you doing?"

Giving my best shot at a witty reply, I said, "I'm playing with my nipples. What does it look like I'm doing?"

We both broke out in laughter before I explained what had happened and what I was doing.

Shaking his head as he walked back toward the door, he said, "I'll give you some alone time."

"Thanks, man. I'll be out of the way in a minute."

"Take your time, dude. Sorry to interrupt."

I finished up, putting Neosporin on each nipple and covering each one with the adhesive end of a Band-Aid I had cut off. The Band-Aids were waterproof, so I knew they wouldn't come off until I wanted them to. Problem solved. No more bleeding nipples. But the fun wasn't over yet.

Back outside, the firefighter was waiting for me. "Bro, I've got a trail name for you. I was going to go with Nips, but given your background and the situation, I think Meat Grinder is more appropriate."

"Meat Grinder. That sounds pretty badass. I dig it!" I said, also happy not to be forever known as Nips.

We had some more laughs before I packed up and headed back to the trail. I never saw him again but was happy to have earned a memorable trail name. I hadn't considered the reactions I would get from other hikers when I told them my trail name, though. Coincidentally, I encountered a lot of young, solo women on the trail, and on a few occasions, it became clear that my trail name was unsettling to some of them. A couple of scenarios went something like this:

Five Million Steps **15**

Me, creepy-looking older guy with a scruffy beard, sees another hiker on a remote section of trail: "Hi. I'm Meat Grinder. How's your day going?"

Her, college-age young lady with a look of terror on her face: "Whoa, h-how did you get that name?"

Me, thinking it would be funny: "Not from, like, murdering anyone or anything like that."

Her, with the same look of terror, clearly not thinking what I said was funny: "Wha-what?"

Me: "Just kidding. But seriously, I got it from a guy who caught me in the bathroom rubbing Neosporin on my nipples. They were bleeding. What's your trail name?"

Her: "Um. Okay. I gotta go. Bye."

*Man, this Meat Grinder thing just doesn't seem to be working out. Still better than Nips, though.*

So, after about a week of uncomfortable situations, I shortened my trail name to "Grinder," thinking that would be less creepy, but I soon found that although it seemed to be less unsettling, I was still getting a lot of interesting looks from people when I told them my trail name. Not thinking much of it, I stuck with Grinder.

A couple weeks went by, and I was hiking around a group of three guys in their early twenties. We were all in camp the second night after I met them when one of them asked, "Hey, man, do you know what Grinder is?"

"Of course," I replied.

"Right on," he said. And that was the end of the discussion.

Hiking with them again the following day, I was telling stories about my wife and sons and kept getting strange looks from them until, finally, the guy who asked me if I knew what Grinder meant asked, "Bro, do you really know what Grinder is?"

I said, "Yeah, it's a hot Italian sandwich, but for me, it's more like grinding miles."

All three of them broke out laughing, and one said, "Not even close, bro!"

Over the next few minutes, they schooled me on many things. Most importantly, I learned all about Grindr, the hook-up app. I was fifty years old at the time, was ignorant to the world of hook-up apps, and had no idea that Grindr was even a thing. We all had a good laugh after that; again, you can't make this stuff up. I decided to go back to Meat Grinder.

Although I came to the trail wanting to be just Jay, I was happy to have earned the trail name Meat Grinder, have fun with it, stop taking myself so seriously, and still have the chance to break away from the military identity I had held for so many years.

CHAPTER 3

# HIKE YOUR OWN HIKE

I first saw AYCE (pronounced "Ace") on the trail right outside Warner Springs, California. I had just picked up the second resupply box my family had sent me and left town with a light pack, three days' worth of food to get me the fifty miles to my next resupply. I had prepared several resupply boxes before leaving home so I could have the food and supplies I wanted and not have to rely on the often-limited items in the small towns I passed through.

I saw AYCE in the distance, probably half a mile ahead of me, as I crossed a large prairie with herds of free-range cattle scattered as far as I could see. His bright-red pack swung from side to side as he walked. As I got closer, I noticed his big pack was making him work for every step he took. *That thing is huge! What the heck does he have in there?* were my first thoughts, but despite his labored movement, he was still moving along pretty good. I caught up to him a couple minutes later, right as he dropped his pack to take a break.

"What's up, man? How's it going?" I asked.

"Not too bad. Just setting this beast down for a minute and taking a break."

"Right on. I haven't met you yet. I'm Meat Grinder," I said, reaching out to shake his hand.

Giving me a solid handshake, he replied, "Nice to meet you, Meat Grinder. I'm AYCE."

"Ace, like the bandage?"

"No. AYCE, as in All You Can Eat. I put down two pizzas by myself in Julian. A group of hikers heard the waitress tell me it was a good thing they didn't have a buffet there because I would put them out of business. They gave me my trail name, All You Can Eat, but that shit was too long, so I shortened it to AYCE."

"Dude, that's awesome! It's great to meet you, AYCE. I'm gonna keep moving, but I hope to see you again soon."

"Take care, man. I hope so too."

AYCE was about five and a half feet tall and probably weighed 130 pounds. His pack was easily one-third of his weight and looked enormous when he had it on. It was clean and new, like most of our packs still were at that point, about 115 miles into the hike. I noticed he had a pair of shoes and a pair of Teva sandals hanging on the outside of his pack; two large, heavy Nalgene bottles in the side pockets; and a big fixed-blade hunting knife sticking out of the back pocket of his pack, all telltale signs of an inexperienced hiker. He was out here, though, and over a hundred miles into hiking the PCT, and I was happy to meet him.

I saw AYCE six days later in Idyllwild. I had to stay there for two days to handle some personal business. On my second day, I was in the lobby of the lodge I was staying at when a truck pulled up with a hiker in the bed. At first, I didn't recognize who it was. The guy got out of the truck very slowly, struggled to get his pack out, and limped up to the lobby entrance. Once he was inside, I saw it was AYCE.

"Dude! What's up? It's awesome to see you. How are you?" I asked.

"I'm sucking, bro. This pack is kicking my ass," he said with a look of defeat. "I brought way too much shit. I need to ditch some of it before I get back on the trail. How long have you been here?"

"I got in night before last," I said. "I had to take care of some business for a job I'm taking when I get home. I'm heading back to the trail tomorrow. You hungry? I was about to head to the Mexican place, but I can wait."

"Hell, yeah, man!" he said, now with a big grin. "Can you give me about thirty minutes to check in and clean up?"

"Too easy. I'll meet you right here."

AYCE and I had a great dinner. We discussed all things life and hiking over tacos, enchiladas, and beer. He was a twenty-six-year-old waiter from Iowa. His PCT experience was full of firsts: first time hiking, first time sleeping outside, and first time in the California desert. He'd learned about the PCT from a customer who had hiked it in 2018 and decided he wanted to do it too. So, after a stroke of luck getting a permit, a couple trips to the outdoor store REI in Des Moines, a plane ride to San Diego, and an Uber to Campo, he was on the trail.

He had a rough start, though. The night before AYCE started, he set up his tent for the first time at Camp Lockett—a popular place for hikers to stay near the southern terminus—and left his tent stakes behind when he started his first day. He had to use rocks to hold down his tent until he got to the Laguna Mountain Lodge, forty miles into the hike, and bought new ones. In his excitement, he had also forgotten to get a fuel canister for his stove and used cold water to partially reconstitute his freeze-dried meals for the first four days until he got one at Mount Laguna. He was embarrassed to ask other hikers if he could use one of theirs to boil the water he needed for his meals. He told me they all seemed so confident and skilled and that he felt he wasn't as good as them. He was stuck in the comparison trap. He was probably a bit in over his head when he started, but he was sticking it out, he was learning, and I admired and respected him for it.

On the walk back to the lodge from dinner, I asked, "Is there anything

I can help you with?"

He hesitated, then finally asked, "Can you please take a look at my stuff and maybe give me some pointers? And can you show me what you're carrying if it's not too much of a pain?"

"Too easy, brother. I'd be happy to."

On the large, open patio behind the lodge's lobby, we spent an hour looking at and discussing every piece of gear he had before spending another hour doing the same with mine. I explained why I carried everything I did. I made no recommendations; I just provided some thoughts on each item based on my experiences. I wanted him to think about and decide what would work best for him. AYCE set aside quite a few items to send home the next day. It felt good to help him out, and he was very appreciative.

I had an early day ahead, so after I packed up all of my stuff, I gave him one last piece of advice before I left his room. "Do you, bro. This is your journey, no one else's. Don't get wrapped up in what other people think, the equipment they're carrying, or the miles they're doing. All that matters is what works for you."

"Thanks for helping me, man. And thanks for not treating me like a dumbass. It really means a lot."

I could tell he had a good heart, and he was genuinely appreciative of the time we'd spent together and what I'd shared with him. We'd spent a lot of time focusing on gear, but the most valuable thing I shared with him was the mindset that's so important for anyone on a hiking journey. It revolves around the common trail phrase "Hike your own hike"; in other words, don't compare yourself with others.

If there was one thing I couldn't understand but dealt with the entire hike, it was comparisons.

"How many miles are you doing every day?"

"How much does your pack weigh?"

"How many days will it take you to get to the border?"

"How many zero-days have you taken?"

"Why don't you just shop instead of sending all those resupply boxes?"

The list of comparisons I saw on the trail seemed endless, and in most cases those comparisons added no real value to anyone's experience.

My read on the people I saw comparing themselves with others fell into a few categories. Some were genuinely trying to learn. Some were simply trying to start a conversation. Some lacked confidence and were seeking validation from others. And a few were trying to make themselves feel better by putting others down.

I mean, think about it. How could the weight of my pack improve someone else's experience? Or how could the miles I did in a day diminish someone else's experience? Even if two hikers carried the exact same items, wore the same shoes, ate the same food, and did the same number of miles in the same amount of time each day, they would still have two completely different experiences.

My PCT journey was my own, and only my own, from start to finish. I followed the "Hike your own hike" concept and didn't concern myself with what other hikers were or were not doing. If I wanted to hike over thirty-five miles in a day, it was about me challenging myself or pushing my limits. It wasn't to impress anyone. If I wanted to go as light as possible, with the bare minimum amount of equipment, it was about me seeing how far I could push my comfort tolerance. Again, it wasn't about anyone else.

People with different gear, doing different miles, stopping in different towns, and using a different resupply strategy than I was didn't concern me one bit. I was happy to be on the same trail with them; happy to meet and talk and learn about them; happy to have coffee, beer, and tacos with them. I loved sharing the journey with so many different and interesting people.

The saddest effects of comparisons I saw on the trail were the people who perceived themselves as failures because they believed they weren't as good as other hikers. This was especially true for the people who were

Five Million Steps  **23**

forced or decided to end their PCT journeys before reaching the terminus. Hearing comments like "I didn't make it all the way to the Canadian border" or "I only hiked five hundred miles" when the person saying it viewed their achievements as failures always got to me. Life happens. Injuries happen. Some people get all they want out of their PCT journey in less than 2,650 miles. Some people discover they are more passionate about something other than hiking and leave the trail to pursue a greater passion.

I didn't view anyone leaving the trail as a failure. I viewed their PCT experiences only as successes. So what if someone didn't hike all the way to the Canadian border? The experiences they gained, the things they learned about themselves, the people they met, and the views they saw were the most rewarding parts of the experience, whether they went 100, 1,000, or 2,650 miles. And to the thoughts of people "only" hiking however many miles and viewing it through a lens of failure: again, it's about the experiences and moments along the way, not the miles. Shifting one's perspective from "I only hiked five hundred miles, so I didn't get to experience . . ." to "I hiked five hundred miles and got to experience . . ." can flip the feeling of failure to a sense of success. Our PCT journeys are our own. We, not others, define what our success looks like.

I had also seen the downsides of comparisons throughout my air force career. I spent many years comparing myself with others, especially at the beginning of my career. I was focused on the opportunities others received when I should have been creating the right opportunities for myself. I focused on what others got on their evaluations instead of being honest with myself, improving my weak areas, and accepting the evaluation ratings I deserved. I focused on how quickly others were getting promoted when, in reality, they deserved to be promoted more than I did, and maybe it wasn't the right time for me to wear another stripe.

It wasn't until twelve years into my career that I stopped comparing myself so much with others. I was interviewed and selected for an assignment in special operations, and a member of the interview panel later told me, "One of the reasons we selected you is that you'll bring thoughts, skills, and experiences to our team that no one else has. You're going to see things that others won't. You're going to approach problems differently. One of our greatest strengths is our differences. You're going to make us stronger."

He was a skilled, experienced, and well-respected special operator who had been in that community for decades. I'd been intimidated to have him on the panel. That brief, but meaningful, interaction gave me a huge boost of confidence and encouraged me to stop comparing myself with others and set my own path.

I also soon learned that pursuing my passions, not worrying about evaluations and promotions, and caring for people and my family made the experiences more rewarding and memorable. And to my surprise, the opportunities and promotions came quickly once I stopped worrying about them.

When I moved into new positions, I made them mine. I didn't concern myself with what the last person did. That didn't matter anymore. It was mine now. It was a different time, different people, different environment, different challenges. So I owned it. Blaming the person before me for anything was pointless. And similar to a hiking journey, no two people's careers will be the same. We could be assigned to the same places, promote at the same time, go to the same schools, and get the same accolades and awards, and we would still have two completely different experiences.

And also similar to a hiking journey, those who accomplished all they wanted during their air force career—whether it was four years, twenty years, or more—should be incredibly proud. Sometimes a life event will be more important than a promotion, position, or even continued service, and that's okay. People's accomplishments and experiences and the people they met along the way are the best parts of the journey. And everyone's journey is their own.

Five Million Steps **25**

I hiked my own hike on the trail and in my career and was rewarded with some of the greatest experiences and memories of my life. And I would do them both all over again.

CHAPTER 4

# SEEN THROUGH A DIFFERENT LENS

I finally arrived in Big Bear Lake, California, just before one o'clock. The Uber driver dropped me off at the hotel where I had reservations for two nights. I had hoped to get into town earlier that morning before the heat kicked in, but everything I had planned for that day started to fall apart as soon as I stepped off the trail.

I reached the Eye of God trailhead just before 8:00 a.m. The trailhead intersects with California Highway 18, about ten miles northeast of the city. I had camped five miles from the trailhead the previous night and started hiking before sunrise to make it to the trailhead and into the city as early as possible.

It was a Saturday, and I thought there would be plenty of traffic heading into Big Bear Lake. I planned to hitch into town, find a coffee shop or café near one of the city's laundromats where I could eat and spend time out of the heat while doing my laundry, go to the grocery store near my hotel to buy all the food I needed to take me to the next town, and get to the hotel with all my chores done right at check-in time.

27

Unfortunately, the easy hitch I'd hoped for didn't work out. There was plenty of traffic coming from the city but hardly any heading toward the city. And the cars heading in the direction I needed to go had no interest in picking up a hitchhiker.

I spent the first hour next to the highway with my thumb out, smiling and waving at every vehicle that passed by, but hardly anyone even glanced at me. Fortunately, I had cellular service. There is a network of people called "trail angels" who support hikers in various ways, typically by giving rides between trailheads and towns, surprising us by providing food in remote areas, and sometimes even letting hikers stay overnight in their homes.

I called three different trail angels who had left their phone numbers in comments on Guthook (now called FarOut), the popular navigation app many hikers use. None answered. I also read on Guthook that sometimes, during the day, Uber drivers were available in Big Bear Lake. I tried to reach one on the app, but none were available, so it was back to trying to hitch. Another hour went by with no luck. I even offered to pay a few people who had parked at the trailhead and were headed out for trail runs or day hikes to bring me into town, but none wanted to delay their plans and give me a ride.

By then, the temperature was rising. As the sun beat down on me, my frustration grew. I got lucky my second time on the Uber app, though, and was able to reserve a ride. The driver was only twenty minutes away. Another PCT hiker I had met a few days before emerged from the trail and asked if he could share the Uber with me. *Lucky him*, I thought. His day was clearly going better than mine. I messaged the driver, and he agreed to bring both of us, but it would now be forty-five minutes until he could pick us up. Still a bit frustrated but happy to have finally secured a ride, the other hiker and I found shade under a tree and waited until our Uber arrived.

The ride into town was quick. We dropped off the other hiker at his hotel before heading to mine. Despite my delay, I arrived two hours before check-in time and expected to have to wait to get my room. I hoped to leave my pack there and at least do my laundry at the laundromat across the street and go shopping for my resupply items before checking in. The front-desk agent must have sensed I needed a break when I spoke to her. She allowed me to check in early and even told me I could wash my clothes in the housekeeping laundry room since the hotel had no washers and dryers for the guests to use. My day was finally turning around.

Like most other cheap hotels I stayed in during my hike, my room was small and had only the essentials: a full-sized bed, one nightstand with an old digital clock, a small table and chair near the window, a TV on a small stand, and a lamp with a broken shade in the corner. It looked like nothing in the room had been updated since the eighties, but it was clean and gave me a place to rest and prepare for the next stretch of trail. The hotel was also in the middle of town, and I had easy access to everything I needed before heading back to the trail.

The feeling of the air conditioning in my room was amazing. I had been on the trail for precisely three weeks and had covered 266 miles in the dry Southern California heat. Air conditioning was a luxury I had taken for granted in everyday life for quite a while.

It felt great having my pack off too. The next day would be my third zero-day (day off with no miles hiked) since starting. I was happy with the improvements to my physical conditioning and endurance but was still contending with some of the aches and pains that come with starting a long hike. I was looking forward to a day to relax and recover.

Since it took longer than expected to get into town, I had run out of water hours ago. I had carried only two liters from camp that morning and finished it all as soon as I reached the trailhead. Another thing I was still getting used to was the amount of water I needed to drink throughout the day to stay hydrated. I hadn't had enough that day, and dehydration was setting in. As tempting as it was to lie down and enjoy the air conditioning,

I grabbed my phone and wallet and headed to the 7-Eleven I'd passed on the ride to the hotel, less than a quarter mile away. I was craving a Dr Pepper for some reason but also wanted new water bottles to replace the ones I'd been using for the past three weeks.

I didn't change my dirty clothes or attempt to clean myself up before leaving. All my clothes were covered in dust and sweat stains. I had worn the same shirt and pants for the last five days, changing only my socks and underwear each morning. I had two pairs of each and would wear one pair each day, wash the other as best I could at a water source, and hang them in camp to dry so I could have a relatively clean and dry set to put on the next morning. I hadn't showered during that time either. My face, neck, and hands were covered in dust that had stuck to the sweat pouring from me throughout the day. I smelled horrible too.

None of those things bothered me, though, as all the other hikers I was around every day looked the same, and we didn't care how dirty we were. A few things I failed to consider were that I was in a city now, I wasn't around only hikers anymore, and not everyone would understand why I looked the way I did.

Walking up to the front of the 7-Eleven, I stopped on the sidewalk just outside the main door and checked how much cash I had in my wallet. If I were low, I would get some from the ATM inside. I had already learned it was always good to have some cash with me on the trail for the trail angels. Although not always expected, it's nice to give a small cash donation to help them continue supporting hikers.

I noticed a car pull up and park in a spot near me as I finished counting my cash. I glanced up and saw it was an Audi SUV. The driver, a well-dressed woman, probably in her late forties, got out and walked toward the entrance.

I opened and held the door for her as she approached. I smiled and said, "Good afternoon."

She stopped before reaching the door, looked me in the eyes, and paused, almost long enough to make it uncomfortable. She gently asked, "Is there something I can help you with?"

"No, thank you," I replied. "I'm just heading in to get something to drink."

She smiled and asked again, "Are you sure there is nothing I can help you with, someone I can call for you, or a place you know of that I can call to get you some help?"

I was confused. I was simply trying to be courteous and hold the door for her. *Why is she asking me all these questions? All I want to do is get my stuff and get back to the hotel and take a shower.* "No. I'm good. But thank you."

She persisted. "You know, it's okay to ask for help. You don't need to be embarrassed."

Then it hit me. *She thinks I'm homeless.*

She was clearly a kind person. She had caring eyes and a warm smile, and there was genuine concern in her voice. She wasn't speaking to me in a degrading tone, and it didn't seem like she was showing me false pity. She chose to stop, find out if I needed help, and offer to get help for me, when she could have easily walked by.

I could have easily walked away too, but her act of kindness warmed my heart, and I felt inclined to explain the situation. I was still holding the door as two customers came out. I let go after they passed and stepped to the side to finish our conversation without blocking the entrance. "I appreciate your offer, ma'am, but I think you may have mistaken me for a homeless person. I'm hiking the Pacific Crest Trail. I started at the Mexican border three weeks ago, and I just got into town. I haven't showered or washed my clothes since I left Idyllwild five days ago, but I'm heading back to my hotel to clean up after this. Thank you for checking on me, but I'm good."

She wasn't buying it. "I've never heard of the Pacific Crest Trail. Are you sure that's a thing? Like I said, it's okay if you're embarrassed—I would still like to help you."

*Man, she's not going to let it go!*

Five Million Steps  **31**

"I'm not embarrassed, ma'am, and again, I appreciate what you're trying to do for me. And yes, the Pacific Crest Trail is a thing."

Shifting tactics, I attempted to lighten the mood and end our exchange without being rude. With a big grin, I said, "You can pay for one of my drinks if you'd like, though. I'd appreciate that."

Not helpful, and a poor choice of words on my part.

Her warm smile turned into a scowl. "I wouldn't feel comfortable buying you alcohol. Is that what got you here?"

*Way to go, dumbass.*

"I came here to get water and a Dr Pepper, not alcohol."

The smile didn't return. I knew at that point our conversation was going nowhere, and I needed to cut it off. "Thanks again, ma'am. I appreciate you. The world needs more people like you. I've gotta get going now. Take care!" And before she could respond, I headed into the store. I got two bottles of water, my Dr Pepper, and an ice cream sandwich. I paid and got out of there as quickly as I could.

Walking back to the hotel, drinking my Dr Pepper, I thought about what had just happened. I had never been in a situation like that, and questions started popping into my mind. *Should I have handled that differently? Was I a jerk to her at the end? Did I mess up her good deed for the day? Would she have helped me if I actually needed it? Should I clean up before doing anything in other towns?*

Back in my room, my focus shifted to my ice cream sandwich, getting cleaned up, and recovering from my dehydration.

I spent the rest of the afternoon preparing for the hundred-mile stretch to the next town. I was starting to get my zero-day flow and becoming efficient in the process of doing my laundry; grocery shopping; cleaning, inspecting, and repairing my gear; and recharging my electronics. I also edited and uploaded my YouTube videos, a project my youngest son had asked me to take on before leaving so I could share my journey with him and my family.

Throughout the day, though, my thoughts returned to the exchange with the lady at 7-Eleven. Why did she choose me? What stopped her from staying in her car or simply walking by? What would have happened if I needed help and accepted her offer? How many people had she helped before? Did I come off as rude or unappreciative? What would I do differently if I could go back in time?

Although I don't believe I've ever been viewed through that lens—mistaken as a homeless person—the experience reminded me of one of my toughest childhood experiences.

I was in sixth grade, a difficult year for me. As is common with kids around that age, we were all starting to realize our differences. We were trying to figure out who we were and how to express ourselves. Social status and the importance of fitting in and belonging became important, things I never had to worry about before. Peer pressure came into play. Clothes, shoes, hair, where you lived, whom you sat with at lunch—all the things that determined whether you were accepted or not.

I noticed that my clothes weren't as nice as most other people's. I sometimes wore the same clothes several days in a row, and they didn't always fit well. I didn't have the nice, expensive shoes that many others did either. The other kids started to notice the differences too, and I felt the looks, saw the fingers pointed at me, and heard the whispers and giggles. Things that weren't important before quickly became a source of worry and made me feel I wasn't as good as everyone else. Things got progressively worse as the school year went on. Toward the end of the year, it seemed that there was nothing I could do to get the target off my back, and just when I thought things couldn't possibly get worse, they did.

At the beginning of each month, my mother gave me twenty dollars cash to pay for my lunches. Even then, making twenty dollars cover an entire month's worth of school lunches was hard. It was a constant stress—not only the money, but always being hungry too. I was a growing kid, and my appetite picked up around that time. As hard as I tried, I sometimes ran out of lunch money before the end of the month. This was one of those months.

One day, while I was at school, my mother checked the envelope in my room where my lunch money was kept. It was empty, and there were still quite a few school days left in the month. She was waiting for me in the kitchen when I got home. I saw she was furious the moment I walked in the door, and I knew things were about to get bad for me.

She gave me one of the worst scoldings of my life up to that point. My mother never hit me, but I remember wishing she had hit me that time just to get it over with. To me, physical pain would have been better than hearing the things she said to me.

In my mind, I had done nothing wrong. I repeatedly tried to explain why I had spent all the money, that I always bought the cheapest things and only a couple items each day, that I was still hungry after lunch, and that even though I tried hard to make it last, the money she had given me just wasn't enough. My words fell on deaf ears. Nothing I said resonated with her. It just seemed to make her more furious. I retreated to my bedroom, frustrated and confused. I didn't understand why we didn't have the money for my lunches or why what I'd done was such a big deal.

I didn't get any lunch money to cover the rest of that month and none the following month, the last of the school year. So I had to figure out how to deal with my predicament: no lunch for about five weeks of school. Bringing things from home wasn't an option. There was rarely anything to bring, and what was there needed to last. The only other option I saw was not eating and hoping no one noticed.

For the first few days, I sat in the cafeteria with no lunch and just talked with the kids I sat around, but it didn't take long for everyone to notice. I quickly learned that "I forgot my lunch money" and "I'm not hungry" weren't going to work for long.

I switched tactics. I asked kids who had food they were about to throw away, "Are you going to eat that?" and was answered with things like "That's gross!" or "Where's your lunch?" I realized that wasn't going to work either. I was starting to draw more attention. Then the looks started. I knew people were watching. I wasn't sure at first what was worse, being hungry or being embarrassed, but it quickly turned out to be the embarrassment.

On to the next tactic: Remove myself from the situation. I stopped going to the cafeteria.

*If they don't see me, they won't know I have no lunch.*

*If they don't know I have no lunch, they won't know I have no money to buy lunch.*

*If they don't know I have no money to buy lunch, they won't know I'm poor.*

*If they don't know I'm poor, maybe some of them will still like me.*

*If they find out I'm poor, none of them will like me.*

Afraid I was going to get caught and get in trouble, I did different things each day to avoid going to the cafeteria. Some days I hid in bathroom stalls. I was never bothered by anyone there, but it felt gross and uncomfortable. Some days I walked the halls the whole lunch period, telling anyone who questioned me that I was going to my locker to get my lunch. Other days I would find an empty classroom to sit in and position myself where no one walking by could see me. Anything to buy time and get past lunch period.

My plan seemed to be working. I was able to avoid the cafeteria for almost two weeks before getting caught. I was hiding in a classroom when the teacher came in and found me. She wasn't one of my teachers, and I had never spoken to her before.

"What are you doing in here?" she asked with a startled look.

Trying to come up with an excuse, stumbling with my words, I said, "I'm sorry. I thought this was Mrs. Bevins's room" and got up to leave.

*Mrs. Bevins isn't even one of my teachers. Why did I say that?*

"Wait a minute, what's your name?" she asked, head tilted to the side and eyes squinting.

Five Million Steps  **35**

"Jason France," I replied nervously, still trying to reach the door.

"Well, Mr. France, this is not Mrs. Bevins's room. And anyway, I just saw her—she's at lunch. Why aren't you?"

Reaching for the door, I said, "I'm sorry. I'm going back to the cafeteria right now."

I was out of the classroom and walking as quickly as I could toward the cafeteria, heart racing from being caught but happy to have gotten away without having to answer too many questions.

It was at the end of lunch period when I showed up at the cafeteria. Most everyone had already left, besides a few who were still finishing their lunches or making their way out. I entered the door near the large trash cans everyone used to throw away their trash. And there, right on top, as if it were carefully placed there just for me, sat an entire piece of pizza, untouched and on a clean plate. I looked around the room—*no one's looking, no one's coming*—and snatched the pizza from the trash. Still standing there, as if it were mine all along and I was just finishing it as I walked out, I scarfed down the square of pizza. No one saw me. *Yes! It worked!*

My next idea hit me. *I can do this every day!*

I thought my idea was brilliant, and it worked for a while. Three days passed with no issues.

But on the fourth day, I got caught. Just as I had done before, I stood at the trash cans and found what I would take, this time an untouched burrito. I looked around to make sure no one would see me. *All clear.* I grabbed the burrito, took a big bite, and looked up to see four students standing in front of me. They were perfectly still and silent, eyes wide open, jaws dropped.

*Where did they come from?*

The silence lasted only a second before they all burst into laughter, and one of them said, "He doesn't just take out the garbage—he eats it!"

To this day, I have never felt as embarrassed and helpless as I did at that moment. I skipped school for the next two days. When I returned, it was

**36** Jason France

back to hiding in the bathrooms and roaming the hallways again during lunch. I didn't go near the cafeteria again that year. Miraculously, as far as I know, word didn't get around about what had happened. Summer break saved me the week after that.

Looking back on my experience in the cafeteria, and the things that led up to it, I remember feeling sorry for myself at first. I remember being angry and thinking that life was unfair. I remember thinking I was a good kid, couldn't help my situation, and didn't deserve to be treated that way. I remember trying to figure out what I needed to do so no one could ever make me feel that way again. And I remember feeling like I was the only one I could depend on since I was left to do and figure out so much on my own as a kid.

But I didn't realize then that it was a foundational event that led to many positive things later in life. Most importantly, it taught me the value of showing empathy to others. It also set me on a path of building my character and ability to help and protect others. It taught me to find and focus on the positive and not allow myself to be consumed by negativity. It taught me to be humble and grateful for the things I have instead of being upset about what I don't have or being jealous of what others do. It helped me develop my bias for action and ability to "close the gap" between bad and good situations and to constantly improve my position.

I got my first job shortly after that, delivering newspapers early in the mornings during the summer and into the school year. I later worked on farms in the summers, picking flower bulbs and berries so I could help buy clothes for the school year. When I turned sixteen and was old enough to find a regular job, I worked as much as I could, working as a gas station attendant; a dishwasher, bus boy, and waiter at a local restaurant; a construction site laborer; and eventually a produce stocker at the biggest grocery store in town before entering the air force. I was earning money to help take care of myself and learning the importance of a strong work ethic, attention to detail, the rewards of hard work, and how to connect with people and communicate with them.

My encounter with the lady in Big Bear Lake was special to me. It brought back the memory of a difficult, but important, event in my past that helped make me a better person. And the more I thought about the encounter, the more I appreciated what had happened. I'm glad she chose me, and I'm glad I had the experience. It reminded me of everything I have to be grateful for: I have a family who loves me and friends who love me, I just finished a career full of incredible experiences with incredible people, and I was fulfilling my childhood dream of hiking the Pacific Crest Trail. She may have thought she'd come across someone experiencing hard times and needed help, but the person she was really looking at, at that very moment, was the richest man in the world.

CHAPTER 5

# DISCONNECTING

I had a short day, only nine miles, after returning to the trail late in the afternoon following a zero-day in Wrightwood, California. I intended to push five more miles but came across a camp too good to pass up. It was on a large flat area near the top of a ridge facing directly east, where the sun would rise the next morning, and it had a view of a deep valley and layers of mountains as far as I could see. After a month of trial and error scouting for campsites, it had everything I was looking for. It was perfect and ended up being my favorite campsite of the journey so far.

I was in my tent at eight thirty, thinking before I fell asleep about how everything was coming together for me and how my time on the trail was helping me in ways I was just beginning to realize. I was finally coming down from the decades of stress that had built up over my career, especially during the last five years in the two positions that demanded the most of me.

When I stepped off the stage at my retirement ceremony, I was beaming with pride. I got to do and see things during my thirty-one years in the air force that many people only dream about. I was stationed at fourteen different bases worldwide, visited thirty-five countries, served alongside incredible people, and excelled in some of the highest leadership positions in the military.

39

All of it came at a cost, though. A cost to my physical, mental, and emotional well-being. I had given everything I had to the military and the people I served with, and I was exhausted when I walked off that stage. I was burned out and stressed. My anxiety was high. I was constantly fatigued. I wasn't getting quality sleep. I had difficulty staying focused. I wasn't eating as well as I should have been. I wasn't prioritizing fitness as much as I should. One of my main leadership talking points for years was the importance of self-care, but honestly, I did a terrible job of taking care of myself. I had put others first for so many years that I had forgotten the importance of caring for myself.

As my responsibilities increased throughout my career, I became accustomed to taking away things from myself so I could pour more into others. I didn't see the toll my career had on me at the time, but disconnecting from it all on the trail helped me realize the effects and, most importantly, recover from the years I had neglected myself.

The improvements to my physical well-being were the most obvious and immediate. The newness of the trail had faded, and I had discovered my routine. The initial aches and pains were gone, and I had my "trail legs" under me. My body was efficient in all ways. My daily water and calorie intake was dialed in. I found the perfect pace where my heart rate, breathing, and energy output were all synchronized. I was covering greater distances each day, even as the terrain got tougher. The time it took me to recover after hard climbs was reduced to seconds instead of minutes. I felt stronger than I ever had and often wondered, *How can I feel this good when I am putting my body through so much?*

The improvements to my mental and emotional well-being were deeper and took longer to realize. My anxious brain was still spinning for weeks. And my newfound quiet was very loud in the beginning.

When I retired, I was suffering from connection fatigue. Our organization had people and resources all over the world, and I needed to remain connected twenty-four hours a day. I accomplished that through a combination of devices and systems. In my office I had unclassified and secret computers and phones. I accessed a top secret computer and phone in a secure facility near my office. I carried two work cell phones when I was away from my office, one unclassified and the other secret. And finally, I had a tablet at my house when I needed to work on classified things from home. All in all, I communicated with people in fifteen ways via phone, email, text, chat, video, and professional social media accounts. Just being responsive was sometimes a challenge. On a good day, when all the systems were working properly, I could easily spend over an hour sifting through the messages I received on the various platforms, and even longer responding to everything.

Despite no longer having or needing those things, recovery from my connection fatigue came much slower than I'd hoped. I'd had people who relied on me, immediate access to enormous amounts of information, and was attached to devices for so long that for the first few weeks on the trail, I constantly felt I was missing something important. Phantom notifications from devices I wasn't even carrying, waking up in the middle of the night feeling like I'd forgotten to do something or was late in responding to someone, getting anxious when I was in an area without cellular service, and having poor Wi-Fi connection when I was in hotels and restaurants all told me I was addicted to being connected, had been overstimulated for years, and was a prisoner of my devices.

But slowly, as the miles behind me grew, my mind calmed and my anxiety subsided. I found the quiet I was looking for, and being disconnected was no longer a struggle. It was freeing. I started to appreciate the absence of devices, using them only for what was necessary for my journey: capturing photos and video, communicating with my family through my inReach satellite communicator, getting weather data, and navigating the trail with various apps.

I soon realized I was more focused, less distracted, more in tune with my surroundings, connecting better with other people on the trail, and had become better connected with myself. I had downloaded music, audiobooks, podcasts, and movies on my phone before I left, and I realized after a month that I hadn't listened to any of it. I was perfectly content with the sounds of nature, my breath, and my footsteps. I hadn't thought about it before hiking the PCT, but people pay a great deal of money to listen to recordings of the sounds I was immersed in and see the views I was surrounded by through relaxation, meditation, and anxiety-reducing apps, audio collections, and videos. I was getting it all in real time and for free.

My clarity and memory became sharper without the distractions and mental clutter I had before. My sleep improved, and I no longer woke up with racing thoughts or struggled to fall back asleep. I was getting ten hours some nights, not because of the physical work I was putting in but rather from the reduced mental and emotional effort I had to exert. I'd conditioned myself to operate with limited sleep for years and believed I was performing to my full capacity and potential. But the truth was, the poor sleep habits I had developed were preventing me from performing to my full ability. Functioning with limited sleep was a badge of honor in some military circles, and something many bragged about, including me.

I also found that disconnecting from social media and the news improved my mental and emotional well-being. I didn't fully realize how overwhelmingly negative social media and the news had become, or how much they affected me, until I stepped away from them. It felt good to be free of their influence. I started to see people differently, I began to listen differently, and I started to understand differently when I was out of the reach of the media and its influence. My optimism came back stronger after, admittedly, it had slipped. The improvements to my physical, mental, and emotional well-being while on the PCT brought me back to my true self and was exactly what my soul needed.

• • •

I was awakened by the sun at 5:40 a.m. after sleeping through my alarm. I had planned to wake up at 4:30, pack up camp, and enjoy my coffee and breakfast while watching the sunrise, but I was dead to the world and didn't hear the alarm on my watch. The sun had just started to peek over the mountains directly in front of my camp when it woke me up.

I unzipped the doors of my tent and enjoyed the beautiful sunrise from under my quilt. I felt no pressure, no stress, and no anxiety. I was disconnected. The most important decision I had to make at that moment was which cookie to choose for breakfast, snickerdoodle or white chocolate macadamia. I went with the snickerdoodle.

I was on a high from passing the four-hundred-mile mark the day before. I knew it was going to be another awesome day, my thirtieth day on the trail.

# CHAPTER 6

# GRATITUDE

I left Tehachapi loaded with enough food to make it 130 miles to Kennedy Meadows, the end of the 700-mile desert section and the beginning of the Sierra. I had planned on taking six days to cover the distance. Knowing I would soon be leaving the desert and moving into the mountains felt great, but I also knew I would miss it. The desert was a beautiful place. I loved its landscape and expansive views, the smells of the vegetation (especially sage and creosote), the vibrant colors of the sky during sunrises and sunsets, and the experience of hiking in moonlight or camping underneath the stars when there was no moon. The desert also taught me valuable lessons, particularly at the beginning, when I learned how to take care of myself and my gear in its unforgiving conditions. The desert made me strong and prepared me for the challenges I knew I would face in the mountains. I was grateful for all it had provided me.

I had taken a zero-day in Tehachapi the day before, and like every other zero-day, I rested, ate as much as I could, and prepared myself for another long stretch. Also like every other zero-day, it seemed like more work than a day of hiking, and I was ready to get back on the trail and make my way to Kennedy Meadows.

While in Tehachapi, I learned of more hot weather ahead. California had just begun feeling the effects of what would be a summer of record-breaking temperatures. Knowing I was a PCT hiker, many locals warned me of the dangerous conditions. I saw warnings on the news and the weather app on my phone too. I had been in the desert for almost six weeks, though, and felt acclimated and prepared for the conditions, so I didn't worry much about the warnings.

The first two days on the trail were uneventful but brutal. The water sources were sparse, and the temperatures were the highest I had hiked in so far. Despite being acclimated, I felt the fatigue building from the extreme heat and the weight of my pack. It was filled with food and the extra water I had to carry to stay hydrated between water sources. Sometimes the weight of the water alone was over twelve pounds.

Just before noon on the third day, I stopped at a water cache at Bird Spring Pass. It was the last water source for the next twenty miles, so I took a long break there, drank two liters of water, and loaded up with five liters for the hike to Walker Pass. The trail angels who maintained the water cache had also left a cooler with beer, sodas, and snacks. Everything inside the cooler was warm, but I couldn't pass up a free beer, so I enjoyed a warm Pacífico while I took my last few minutes of rest. Two other hikers, a couple from New Jersey, showed up as I prepared to leave. They needed a break from the heat and had arranged for a trail angel to pick them up at the cache and take them to a nearby town. They offered to let me join them, but I didn't want to fall behind on the time I had planned to get to Kennedy Meadows.

The climb out of Bird Spring Pass was punishing. It was completely exposed, and the early afternoon sun was beating down directly on me. It was a constant series of steep switchbacks for miles. I stopped a few times when I came across lone trees to catch a break in any bit of shade that was available. The trees were so small that the shade only covered half of my

**46** Jason France

body at a time, but the breaks were still helpful, even if only in my mind. Continuing the climb, I got more frustrated with the heat, the soft, sandy trail slowing me down, and all the extra water I was carrying. I was nearing the breaking point for the first time on the trail.

Nearing the top of a ridge, after over four miles of climbing, I took another break under the only tree providing shade for as far as I could see. I threw down my pack, slammed my trekking poles to the ground, and plopped down on the trail with my back against the tree. That was the first and only time I lost my cool on the trail. All I could think about was *Why the hell didn't I take that ride?* I checked the map on Guthook to see what was coming up: two small campsites within the next mile. *Way too early to camp—I'll just continue to bake in the sun. But I need a break from this heat.*

Looking for other options, I saw that seventeen miles ahead was Walker Pass, and there were three towns relatively close by: Onyx, Lake Isabella, and Kernville. *Yes! Tomorrow I'll get out of this heat!* I also saw comments on Guthook from people who had difficulty getting a hitch from the pass and recommended contacting one of the local trail angels for a ride. By a stroke of luck, I had cellular service where I was sitting and got on the social media page for the local trail angels. I posted a request to see if anyone could pick me up at the pass the following evening and bring me to Kernville, the town with the best services of the three. I didn't see many responses to other hikers' posts, so I wasn't expecting one either, but I left my cell phone and inReach number anyway.

Within minutes, while still sitting next to the trail, I received a text from a trail angel. She agreed to pick me up, but it had to be first thing in the morning; she wasn't available later in the day. I responded quickly, thanking her and confirming I would be there to meet her. I was so happy that I screamed, "Hell yeah!" at the top of my lungs. I also booked a hotel room in Kernville while I still had cell service.

Doing the quick math in my head, I realized I would have to put in

Five Million Steps **47**

some hard work to make it to Walker Pass in time. I had already hiked ten miles that day, it was one o'clock, and the pass was still seventeen miles away. I hadn't hiked that far in a single day yet, but I wasn't going to pass up the opportunity to get a day in town to cool off. With my spirits lifted and frustration subsiding, I hit the trail again to knock out my biggest day yet.

I arrived at Walker Pass campground just as it was getting dark. I was exhausted, and I had no water left, drinking the last sip an hour before arriving. Fortunately, there was a water cache at the campground, so I had all I needed to start rehydrating after the incredibly tough day. Four other hikers I knew had arrived at the campground earlier. They were seated together at a picnic table in the middle of the campground. They greeted me with a cold beer, one of the best I had on the trail. One of them had hitchhiked into Onyx, got a twelve-pack from the gas station there, and brought it back to the campground. We shared stories, laughs, and more beers as we finished our dinners and retreated to our tents. I was the only one heading into town the next morning.

I set up camp at almost midnight, using my headlamp. My legs were cramping from dehydration and everything I had put them through that day. I could barely set up my tent without my hamstrings knotting up. Not only was it the biggest day for me in mileage, but it was physically and mentally the hardest day of the hike so far too. All I could think about was getting a day out of the heat. I fell asleep with twitching legs and was awakened twice that night with cramping hamstrings.

Mary, the trail angel, picked me up at eight o'clock sharp the next morning. The temperature had already climbed to eighty-five degrees. It was going to be another scorcher. I was excited to see her car coming up the gravel road and to see her smiling face as she pulled up. I knew immediately that Mary was a kind soul. The first thing she did when she got out of her car was thank me for contacting her as she gave me a huge hug. She handed me a cold bottle of Gatorade and asked, "How many other hikers are here?"

**48** Jason France

Most had left before I woke up to get as many miles in as they could before the heat of the day kicked in. "I only saw three other tents this morning. The others that were here last night already left."

"You can put your pack in my trunk," she said. "I'm going to see if they need anything."

She had been to the campground many times before and knew her way around. She grabbed a plastic grocery bag full of bottles of Gatorade and walked toward the center of the campground as I put my pack in the trunk. Waiting for her to return, I relieved myself in the bushes nearby. It was the first time I had peed since the afternoon before. Those twenty-seven miles had worn me out, and I knew it would probably take a couple days to get fully rehydrated again. The Gatorade was precisely what I needed to start that. I stretched my legs in preparation for the hour-long ride to Kernville and was happy not to feel any cramps coming on.

Mary came back empty-handed after checking on the other hikers. "Everyone is good. You ready to go?"

"Yes! And I can't tell you enough how much I appreciate you helping me out."

"You're very welcome. I need to make a stop on the way to town. I hope you don't mind," she said.

"Not at all. I'm in no rush. I'm just happy to get a break from the heat today."

And with that, we were on our way. Mary and I had a great conversation on the way to Kernville. I learned that she had been a trail angel for PCT hikers for fifteen years and had hiked all the trails in the area. She knew the PCT well and the challenges that hikers faced in the desert. She told me interesting stories about other hikers she had met and gave me the history of the places we passed on our drive. I shared some of my trail stories too.

She also told me about her good friend Dan, another local trail angel who had been taking care of hikers for over thirty years. The stop that she

Five Million Steps **49**

told me we had to make was at Dan's house. She had spoken to him the night before, and he wanted Mary and me to stop by for breakfast. I was blown away by the fact that two people I had never met were so kind as to give me a ride into town and a homemade breakfast.

Dan had a small ranch on a five-acre piece of property among about a dozen similar ranches. When Mary and I pulled up, he was sitting on his porch in the shade of the overhang. After greeting us, he welcomed us inside to escape the heat. He showed me around his modest home while Mary went to the kitchen to start cooking our breakfast. His home was sparsely decorated with rustic decor, trinkets, and old photos on the walls. He had great stories to go along with each of the photos, many about the hikers he had helped over the years. His wife had passed away over a decade ago, and he lived alone. It was clear that he was excited to host us, and I was grateful for his hospitality.

I went into the kitchen to help Mary. She had just started making scrambled eggs and ham. "Hey, Jay, can you drop some bread in the toaster and pour us all some orange juice?"

"Absolutely!" I said, happy to contribute.

Dan overheard and shouted from the other room, "We're gonna have to skip the toast today. I'm out of bread."

I thought nothing of it. I was more appreciative of the time I had with him and Mary and their hospitality. Breakfast was a bonus. As I got out the quarter-full bottle of orange juice, I saw that the rest of the refrigerator was nearly empty. Mary was cooking all the eggs and ham that Dan had. There was nothing left in the fridge but a few condiments and what appeared to be two restaurant take-out boxes. He was giving me what little he had. I felt guilty but also incredibly appreciative of the selflessness he was showing to a total stranger.

Mary had to drop me off and get to her afternoon commitment, so we hurried through our breakfast, but not without more great stories from Dan.

**50**  Jason France

I insisted on washing the dishes before leaving, and Mary kindly allowed me a few minutes to do so while she continued the conversation with Dan. When I finished and came back out, I learned that she had arranged for Dan to pick me up in Kernville the next morning and bring me back to Walker Pass, another act of absolute kindness. These two amazing people had done so much for me already and were willing to do even more without me even asking.

The drive into Kernville went by quickly. Mary recommended places to eat and where to shop for resupply items before dropping me off at my hotel. I offered her some cash to cover the gas and time she had given me, but she refused, telling me to use it to take care of the next hiker I met who needed help. That was one more example of what a big heart she had and made me even more grateful for all she had done for me. I got another great big hug from her when she dropped me off and gave her one last heartfelt thank-you before she left.

It was too early for me to check into my hotel, but the front desk clerk allowed me to leave my pack behind the counter, handed me a towel, and told me I was free to use the swimming pool until check-in time. It was 104 degrees outside, and I'm not sure she realized what a gift that simple gesture was, given all I had endured the past few days.

Fortunately, there were large trees around the pool, providing shade to the deck and a portion of the pool. I used a garden hose near the fence to wash off the dirt and grime from my legs and shorts before getting into the water. I hadn't showered in four days, and despite doing my best to clean myself before Mary picked me up, I was still pretty nasty and dirty. The pool was amazing, and I had it all to myself for an hour and a half before the clerk came to let me know my room was ready. It was hard for me to get out of the water and back into the heat.

After checking in, I showered, started my laundry in the hotel laundry room, and walked around the small town of Kernville, where the acts of

Five Million Steps   **51**

kindness from strangers continued and my gratitude intensified. A gentleman paid for my cappuccino and bowl of ice cream at a café. He had hiked the PCT in 2005 and easily picked me out of the crowd as a fellow PCT hiker. We shared some trail stories before he left. After that, I stopped by a fly shop to pick up some local flies. My Tenkara fly rod was waiting for me at Kennedy Meadows, and I needed some flies for the mountain section. One of the local fishermen was in the store the same time I was and insisted on paying for my flies after hearing me talk about fishing in the Sierra. Everyone I ran into in Kernville was incredibly kind, and it all came at the perfect time, when I needed it the most.

Although the acts of kindness by Mary and Dan, and so many great people I met in Kernville, were some of the best I experienced throughout my journey, there were countless other acts as well. Surprise "trail magic" in remote areas—such as drinks and snacks in coolers left next to the trail—rides between trailheads and towns, restaurant tabs picked up by anonymous people wanting to support hikers . . . the list goes on, and all of it was out of the kindness of people's hearts.

The kindness of others has had a profound impact on me for as long as I can remember, long before hiking the PCT. Growing up as an only child of a single mother who didn't work, we had very little and relied primarily on food stamps, the surplus food program, and a local food pantry for most of our food. Our Easter, Thanksgiving, and Christmas meals all came from gift baskets from the food pantry. Volunteers I never got to meet or thank had put the baskets together. Even as a kid, I realized the impact the kindness of others had on me. Those experiences shaped how I care for people and made me grateful for all that I have.

My gratitude for my family became stronger during my PCT journey as well, but in a slightly different way than it had during my time in the military. I thought the physical and mental challenges the trail would throw at me would be the hardest part of my trip. I learned quickly that those weren't the hardest parts at all. It was being away from my wife and sons.

I often questioned my decision to leave them for five months so quickly, less than three weeks after retiring. We had discussed my PCT hike for years, and I knew they fully supported me in all ways, but the question *Should I really be out here right now?* wouldn't get out of my head. After all, before retiring, I had done the math on how long Monica and I had been apart since we met. Between our deployments, schools, and other work-related trips, we had been apart for over six of our twenty years together.

We never viewed our time together as making up for something we had missed, though. Separation was part of our lives as a military family, and we always made the best of our time together instead of dwelling on or being sad about the time we spent apart. Not only did that help us appreciate every moment we had together, but it also helped build optimistic mindsets and independence in our sons.

I noticed early on that being away on my hike was far different from being away during my military career, especially on deployments. As insensitive as it may sound, I tried hard not to let thoughts about my family occupy my mind when I was deployed. My view was that I needed to focus on taking care of myself and the people around me, performing the mission I was sent to do, paying attention to all the inherent dangers associated with what I was doing, and getting my people and myself home safely. My time to think about and connect with my family was usually regimented: a video call once a week, emails, phone calls before or after work, and looking at photos, letters, or cards before going to sleep. That's what I had to do to stay sharp.

I didn't have to concern myself with those things on the PCT, though. I was free to think about my family as much as I wanted, whenever I wanted, and oddly enough, it hurt a little more being away from them on the trail than during a deployment. More time to think about them without distractions made the pain of missing them stronger. But that time without distractions also allowed me to notice more of the little things. The smiles and laughs we shared during our FaceTime calls warmed my heart more than ever. The memories of experiences we shared in the past were clearer and more meaningful. And thoughts of what our future might bring were limitless.

We were able to connect more often too, several times a day on most days. I loved texting Monica photos of things that made me think about her: flowers, heart-shaped rocks, and butterflies. I loved sending my sons messages and photos to let them know I was thinking about them too. And it felt great to receive messages from them throughout the day, always seeming to arrive exactly when I needed them the most. They were with me on the trail, and I came back even more grateful for the incredible family I have.

CHAPTER 7

# CONNECTION

Dan dropped me off at Walker Pass campground just after one in the afternoon. He'd picked me up from my hotel in Kernville earlier that morning, and we stopped at his ranch before the thirty-minute drive to the pass to fill up fifteen one-gallon water bottles for the water cache at the campground. It felt good to help Dan after all he had done for me, and to help my fellow hikers, as that water cache is in the middle of a long dry stretch, with no water on the trail for more than ten miles in the direction I was headed. All of us were still trapped in a heat wave that had been torturing us for the past week, and that cache was a lifesaver.

I was met with a blast of heat when I stepped out of Dan's truck. It was already ninety-seven degrees, and there were still a couple hours until the hottest part of the day. I'd been spoiled with air conditioning during the drive. I was somewhat refreshed after my zero-day but still felt the fatigue that had grown from being outside in the record temperatures, day in and day out, for weeks. My excitement to have only fifty miles left in the desert section had me in a great mood, though, and I was ready to make my final push to Kennedy Meadows and into the mountains, regardless of the heat.

Dan and I were met by eight exhausted hikers and another trail angel

55

at the campground. They were gathered at a picnic table, where the water cache was located, all huddled under the patch of shade the small roof over the table provided. All the water bottles were empty, and the group was ecstatic to see we'd brought full ones. Everyone pitched in to unload the full bottles and put the empty ones in the back of Dan's truck so he could refill and bring them back the next day. The other trail angel had brought sandwiches, chips, fruit, and sodas that the group had nearly devoured before we arrived. I wanted to stick around, spend time with the other hikers, and have one last snack, but I couldn't delay the inevitable any longer; it was time to get back on the trail. I said my goodbyes to the group, thanked Dan one last time for all he had done for me, and headed north, alone again.

It was a steep, slow, and steady climb for the first eight miles leaving Walker Pass. Most of the trail was open and exposed, with few trees to provide any shade. The sights were incredible, though, with desert views and low mountains for miles all around. I could see the trail winding around the terrain in front of me for miles in some areas too. As I climbed, I walked through small patches of pinyon pine and manzanita trees, and the smells were amazing. A mild breeze and occasional cloud cover helped make the heat and sun feel less brutal.

As I neared the top of my big climb for the day, I saw another hiker ahead of me in the distance, sitting next to the trail in a tiny patch of shade near some boulders. As I got closer, I recognized him from Tehachapi, almost a hundred miles ago. It was James. I'd met him in the laundromat in town during a zero-day.

Three things stuck out in my mind when I thought about our conversation at the laundromat. First, he was an honest but bold guy. When I introduced myself, he said, "That is just the dumbest shit. Why would you want anyone calling you Meat Grinder?" Second, he refused to take a trail name. "There's no fucking way I'll ever have a trail name. My name is James." And third was how messed up his feet were. He was wearing flip-flops in the laundromat, and I could see that the skin all around his ankles and heels had blistered and peeled off. I had never seen anyone's heels in that condition. They looked burned: bright red, oozing fluid, and dark spots where blood had dried. The skin on all his toes was in a similar condition too: all had blistered, with skin torn off. He was limping and wincing with every step, and I couldn't believe anyone with feet in such bad condition was still hiking.

I liked James from the moment we met, though. Anyone willing to come at me about my trail name the way he did is an instant friend in my view. I felt bad about how messed up his feet were and thought he should probably get off the trail until he healed, but I also admired his determination to keep pushing on.

As I got close enough to see him clearly, I could tell he wasn't the same James I remembered from Tehachapi. His expression told me he wasn't the confident, cocky young man I'd met a week ago; he was in bad shape.

"Hey, James. What's up?" I said with a cheery voice and a smile, hoping to lighten his obvious bad mood.

Glancing up at me quickly and then back at the ground with no sign of a smile, he replied, "I'm done, man. I can't do this shit anymore."

"What's going on?" I asked as I set my pack down and sat on a rock next to him.

"My feet are trashed. I'm done. I'm going home," he said quietly, still looking at the ground.

Sensing his desperation but hoping to get a smile or a laugh, I said, "Well you can't just quit here. We're in the middle of nowhere. Do you want me to text your mom so she can come pick up her baby boy? I already have her number."

Nothing. Not even a chuckle. *Damn, he really is in bad shape.* "Have your feet gotten any better since Tehachapi?"

"No. They're still the same."

Five Million Steps    **57**

"What do you mean 'the same'? There's no way you've come this far if they're still that messed up. Have they healed at all? Looking any better than they did at the laundromat?"

"I don't know. I haven't taken my socks off in three days. It hurts too much. The last time I took them off, it ripped off some of the scabs. I don't even want to look."

*Three days?* This was gonna be bad. "Dude, your feet were a mess. They've got to be infected if you haven't been cleaning them. Let me take a look."

"No, man. If I take off my shoes and socks here, I'm not moving again today. I'll check my feet when I get to camp."

*Get to camp? So he's staying on the trail?*

Confused by his conflicting comments, I asked, "So are you going back to Walker Pass and leaving, or are you continuing to Kennedy Meadows? I'm camping in about six miles. What about you?"

"No. Shit. I might as well try to keep going. Same place, I think. Next water source. At the bottom of the big descent coming up."

*Okay, he's not going to quit today.*

"Yep. Same place. All right. We've got plenty of daylight left. I'll hike with you." James finally looked up, and I got a smile from him. "Now quit feeling sorry for yourself, and let's go."

We took it slow during our descent into camp, but the time seemed to go by quickly. James's pace picked up once he was up and moving, and I could tell he wanted to go faster since I was with him. I took the lead, though, and kept our pace nice and slow, not wanting his pride to take over and make his injuries worse.

We talked the entire six miles to camp. I wanted to keep his mind on something other than the pain I knew he had to be feeling, but I also enjoyed being around another person after hiking alone for so long. We shared a lot about each other, and I learned things about James that I never would have guessed from our initial encounter at the laundromat. He was twenty-three years old and had graduated college the year before with a bachelor's degree in civil engineering, a path that his father, who was the same age as me, wanted him to pursue. James had no passion for it. He wanted to earn his degree in exercise science and eventually become an exercise physiologist—a dead-end career according to his father.

After graduating, he chose, against his father's wishes, to take a break from school instead of immediately starting his master's degree. He wanted to hike the PCT in hopes of discovering what direction to take in life. Should he follow his desire to become an exercise physiologist, follow the path that would please his father but make himself miserable, or discover a completely new path in life?

His father was furious at his decision to hike the PCT. His mother, on the other hand, fully supported him. James was an only child, and his mother had always encouraged him to follow his passions. His parents' different views of what James should do with his life was but one item on the long list of reasons that drove them to divorce when James was a senior in high school. His father's infidelity was the biggest reason, though. James admitted he was happy that hiking the PCT made his mom proud and infuriated his dad. It was great to see his eyes light up and his smile when he talked about his mom, and I felt for him when he shared his frustrations about his dad.

We reached camp about an hour before sunset. We both set up quickly and filled our water bottles at the nearby spring before I checked James's feet. We were both nervous as we sat beside each other and James propped his right foot up on a rock. As he removed his first shoe, I saw the blood and fluid that had soaked and dried on his sock, some areas stuck to the wounds. The second one was even worse. Once his shoes were off, he slowly peeled off his socks, wincing again in pain as the wool material tore away from where it had dried and bonded to some of his open wounds. It was difficult to even watch. Blood and fluid immediately started to ooze from

Five Million Steps **59**

the spots where his socks had been stuck. I was amazed to see that as bad as his wounds were, none of the areas looked infected. His feet were in horrible shape, but I was expecting much worse, given that he had been wearing the same pair of socks for three days on that hot, dusty stretch of trail.

"You should rinse off as much of the dirt and sweat as you can, dude. I don't see anything that looks like infection, but they're still pretty nasty."

"I don't want to waste the water, bro. I'll be fine."

The tone of his voice told me he was more worried about the pain that washing his feet would cause than using his water. The spring was less than a quarter mile away, an easy trip for me. "I'll get more water for you. You really need to clean your feet."

Knowing I wasn't hearing his excuses, he spat out, "Fine, but you can't tell anyone if I cry," and gave me a nervous half grin.

"Deal. I'll pour the water. You scrub."

His grin disappeared, and his eyes opened wide as I unscrewed the cap of the first water bottle and lifted it above his foot.

"You ready, dude?" I asked.

"Just do it."

He inhaled sharply with a hiss as soon as the first splash of water hit the wounds on his foot. "God damn, that burns!"

"Clean them as good as you can, dude. The quicker you do, the quicker this will be over with."

Getting over the initial shock of the cold water and pain, but hands still shaking, he cleaned his wounds and got off most of the dirt that had accumulated on the first foot. I emptied his second one-liter bottle on the same foot for good measure.

Reaching for both of my water bottles, I said, "See, that wasn't so bad. Ready for the next one?"

He said nothing that time, just lifted his left foot up onto the rock next to the right. Again, I poured two liters of water as he scrubbed the sweat and dirt off. It was as clean as it was going to get.

"Great job, bro. I know that shit hurt. You should put on some Neosporin, let your feet air out as much as possible tonight, and put on your clean socks in the morning."

"My other pair is dirty too, but cleaner than these. I'll just put them on and call it good."

I frowned, glancing at his feet again. Just coming out of town that morning, having done my laundry the day before, I had a clean pair in my pack. I knew I had two new pairs in my resupply box at Kennedy Meadows and that I would be fine wearing the pair I had on for two more days. James hadn't taken a zero in Kernville like I did. His last zero, and the last time he did laundry, was in Tehachapi, a hundred miles back.

"Bro," I said, "I have a clean pair you can have. I have two new pairs waiting for me at Kennedy Meadows. I'm going to the spring to fill up our water bottles, and I'll grab the socks for you when I get back."

James gave me one of the sincerest smiles I saw during my entire journey. "Thanks, Jay. I can't tell you how much I appreciate all of this, man, seriously."

"You're welcome. I know you'd do the same for me."

I refilled our water bottles and returned to camp just as it was getting dark. We chatted some more while we ate our dinners, and I gave James my extra pair of socks before heading to my tent for the night. I fell asleep happy, knowing I got to help someone who needed it, but also that I was able to connect with someone after being solo on the trail for so long.

I woke up before James the next morning. While I broke camp, I heard him snoring loudly in his tent. I wanted to see how he was doing, if he was still thinking about leaving the trail, and to check his feet again. I was itching to get to Kennedy Meadows, to be done with the desert. I wanted to get an early start. But I didn't want to leave without checking on him. Fortunately, he woke up just as I finished putting everything in my pack. I heard him rustling around in his tent and the zipper of his tent door opening. His head poked out. "Good morning, man. What's up?"

"Good morning, brother. How are you feeling?"

Still groggy, eyes puffy, and hair a huge mess: "Much better than yesterday. My feet feel a little better too. Thanks again for sticking with me."

"All good, man. You're very welcome. Do you want to hike together again today? I can wait for you, and we can take it slow into Kennedy Meadows. Only thirty-six more miles!"

"I appreciate it, but I'm going to take my time today and don't want to slow you down. It'll probably take me three days to get there."

I was relieved since I wanted to cover the thirty-six miles in a day and a half, but I also felt bad about leaving him alone. "Are you sure? I can stick with you. It's really not a problem."

"You've done enough, man. If you're still taking a zero at Kennedy Meadows, I hope to see you there before you head out."

"Right on. Just don't ask me to help wash your nasty-ass feet again when you get there. You can buy me a beer, though."

His grin told me things were going to be okay. "Deal. Beers on me."

And with that I was back on the trail, solo again, and on my way to Kennedy Meadows. Just as I had planned, it took me a day and a half to get there. It was an incredible feeling to make it there: seven hundred miles in, the Mojave Desert behind me, and the Sierra Nevada mountain range ahead. About seventy-five other hikers were there when I arrived, all feeling accomplished after making it through the desert and excited to get into the mountains. The beer and drinks were flowing, and everyone in the kitchen was working as fast as they could to keep up with all the orders from the hungry mob.

I reunited with several hikers I had met in the desert. Some were nervous about entering the Sierra since there were reports of deep snow and ice at the higher elevations, and dangerous stream crossings and swarms of mosquitoes at the lower elevations. Most were sticking together in the trail families they had formed, hoping for safety in numbers, especially when negotiating the snowfields and ice and going over the higher passes. I still wanted to hike alone mostly but was happy that I would see other hikers on the trail every day.

After a huge lunch of two double cheeseburgers, fries, a milkshake, and a beer, I set up my tent in the sea of other tents in a wooded area away from the restaurant. With the lingering high temperatures and the constant activity of the other hikers all around me, I knew right away I wasn't going to get much rest on my zero-day. I considered getting back on the trail that same day, but I was worn out from the past three days in the sun and heat. I needed a rest. I also wanted to wait and make sure James arrived all right.

I picked up my resupply box from the restaurant. They allow hikers to send mail there and hold it for them until they arrive. I brought the box outside to an empty picnic table and laid everything out to figure out how to fit it all in my pack. Five days' worth of food, a bear canister to store my food through the mountain section, fishing gear, and some additional clothing for the lower temperatures all added to the things my pack barely held before. Miraculously, I was able to make it all fit. As expected, I had a hard time sleeping in the heat and with the constant activity in camp, but it was nice to be around and feed off the energy of the other hikers.

The following day, my zero-day, was another scorcher, and I spent as much time as possible inside the restaurant. Although the restaurant had no air conditioning, it was still cool. Finishing my typical zero-day tasks took much longer than usual with the huge crowd of hikers there. The entire place was even more packed than the day before. I endured a three-hour wait to use the lone washer and dryer and rushed through one of the quickest showers I've ever taken after waiting in line for my turn at one of the two outdoor showers. I also enjoyed reconnecting with people I knew and meeting new ones, but by the end of the day, I was ready to get back

Five Million Steps **63**

on the trail and have some time alone again.

After another restless night, I was one of the first ones to pack up my camp and head to the restaurant for one final big breakfast. The next restaurant I would see was in Bishop, five days away. I wanted to get as many calories in me before I left and save all the food in my pack for the long stretch. I left my pack outside on the patio, lined up with other hikers' packs that were leaving that morning, then headed inside the restaurant. I ordered an enormous breakfast: a pancake so big it covered an entire plate, and eggs, hash browns, and bacon that covered a second plate. Dozens more hikers started showing up as I waited for my order, and the place was packed with people by the time it arrived.

I brought my breakfast outside to get away from the crowd, and there in front of me, sitting at an empty table and talking on his phone, was James. His pack was next to him, and I could tell he'd just walked up.

He shouted, "Jay! Come say hi to my mom!" before standing up and giving me a huge hug, almost knocking the plates out of my hands.

"Dude, it's great to see you!" I said, trying not to drop my breakfast as I set the plates on the table. "When did you get in?"

"A few minutes ago. I'm FaceTiming my mom. Let me introduce you." He spun around and backed up next to me so we were both in the camera's view. James's mother had a huge smile on her face, and I saw tears in her eyes.

"Hi, James's mom. It's nice to meet you."

Still excited, James continued, "This is the guy I was telling you about. He's the only reason I'm still here."

I was taken aback by his comment. *Only reason he's still here?*

"Thank you for being there for James," his mom told me. "He said he was about to quit until you stayed with him and helped him out."

"It was my pleasure, ma'am. He's a tough dude, and he's kicking butt out here. You've got a lot to be proud of." I saw the pride on her face when I told her that. I saw the pride on his too. "It was nice meeting you, ma'am.

I'm glad I got to meet your son. He helped me through a tough day too, and I appreciate him. I'll get out of here so you can talk to James. Take care."

I picked up my plates again and moved to another table so James could have some privacy for his call. A few minutes later, just as I finished my breakfast, he sat across from me.

"Thanks, dude, for everything. I was seriously about to head back to Walker Pass when you walked up on me. You're the only reason I didn't quit. And those things you said to my mom—thanks for that too. She's been worried about me, and that really helped."

"You're welcome, man. I'm glad we ran into each other again and got to hang out for a bit. And thank you too. It was great to spend some time with you after being solo for so long."

We talked on the patio for a few more minutes before it was time for me to finish my breakfast and get moving.

"How long are you going to stay here?" I asked.

"Two or three days at least, maybe more. This place has everything I need, and I want to let my feet heal some more before hitting the mountains."

"I'm glad you're taking a break. I hope your feet get better. Enjoy your time here—it's a pretty cool place." I gathered my empty plates. "Take care, brother, I hope to see you down the trail."

"Right on, bro. I hope so too."

Back on the trail after leaving Kennedy Meadows, I thought about how quickly James and I had connected. It was an example of how you never know what is going on in someone's life until you take the time to build a connection. I also thought about the FaceTime call with his mom and our conversation on the patio. They both reinforced something I'd always known but rarely got to see so clearly: the difference one moment can make in someone's life. Several of those moments have shaped my life, but one, from when I was in elementary school, stands out as the most impactful.

I spent a lot of time alone at home as a kid. That meant I was usually free to do whatever I wanted. I had grown to be independent and, at the time, didn't think much of it. That was what normal looked like for me. For as long as I can remember, on most days I would get up, get ready, and get to school on my own. I had a similar routine when I got home from school: ride my bike around our neighborhood or to the beach, fish on the piers downtown, play in our yard or in my room, prepare my own dinner and eat by myself, get my things ready for the next day, and get to bed on my own. Some days my mom was around, and some days she wasn't.

One day in fifth grade, I came home to a quiet house: nothing out of the ordinary. I listened in the kitchen to see if I could hear my mom but heard nothing. We hadn't talked much in the previous few days; she hadn't been feeling well and spent most of her time in her bedroom. I wanted to check on her before riding my bike to the beach.

I knocked on her bedroom door. "Mom, are you in there?"

I waited a few seconds and got no response. I knocked again, louder this time. "Mom, are you in there?"

That time she responded, "Just go play."

Typically, I would do as I was told and leave, but her voice was different. "Can I come in, Mom?"

A few seconds passed. "No, just go and play." Her voice was weak and shaky.

"Are you okay?" I asked.

"I'm fine, just leave me alone and go play."

I knew something was wrong, though, so I cracked the door open slightly and asked again, "Mom, are you okay?"

I heard nothing, so I opened the door a little bit more, just enough to peek my head inside and see her lying on her bed. The sight of her scared me so bad that I couldn't move or speak. I had not seen a dead person before, but I thought I was looking at one at that moment. She was lying on her side, facing me. Her skin was gray, and there were dark spots under her eyes, which were barely open. Her lips were dry and cracked, and her hair was matted and looked like it had been soaked in sweat and dried over and over. I didn't know then, but she had developed a kidney infection so bad that they were beginning to fail.

I was afraid to get any closer or to touch her. I wanted to run away, but I couldn't.

She said again, barely moving her lips and clearly struggling to speak, "I'm okay. Just go and play."

I jumped when I heard her speak, and I knew I had to move if I was going to get help. Our only phone was hanging on the kitchen wall, a rotary phone with a coiled cord that could reach about ten feet when fully extended. I knew I wouldn't be able to keep an eye on my mom and talk on the phone at the same time, but I had to leave her. I ran to the kitchen and called 911.

I don't remember all the details of the phone call, but I remember having difficulty getting the words out to explain to the dispatcher what was happening. I remember her soothing voice telling me I was doing a great job. I remember her asking questions like what grade I was in and what was the name of my favorite teacher. I remember her updating me on how long until the ambulance arrived. Soon I heard sirens in the distance.

Everything happened quickly after that. A police officer and two paramedics arrived at the same time. I thought they would come to the side door, which was closest to the driveway where they parked and visible from where I stood in the kitchen. They all went to the front door instead and knocked hard and fast while ringing the doorbell at the same time.

I couldn't move again, though. My legs were frozen, and I felt like I was going to throw up. The dispatcher heard the commotion in the background and asked me to put down the phone and go open the door, but I told her I couldn't move. She asked me if it was okay for her to tell them to come inside, and I said yes. A couple seconds later, all three of them were inside. I pointed the paramedics to my mom's bedroom, and the police officer stayed with me.

Just as the police officer started talking to me, two firefighters entered the front door. The police officer pointed them toward my mom's bedroom, and one of the firefighters smiled at me as he passed and said, "Hey, bud, we're going to take good care of your mom, okay?"

The police officer told me to hand him the phone so he could talk to the dispatcher. I was in full panic mode from all the activity and wasn't about to hand that phone to anyone. The dispatcher was the only person giving me comfort. I saw the frustration on the police officer's face when I repeatedly refused to hand him the phone. I started crying again, and that frustrated him even more.

The firefighter who had smiled at me heard the exchange between me and the police officer and came back into the kitchen. He asked if I would let him talk to the dispatcher so he could let her know that I was okay, and that they would be taking my mom to the hospital soon. He also told me that he would return the phone as soon as he was done talking with her. His voice was calm, he was still smiling, and he had a look of sincerity in his eyes that made me feel like I could trust him. I reluctantly handed him the phone. He kept his word and handed the phone back to me after speaking with the dispatcher. He also told me the paramedics were taking good care of my mom and that he would stay with me until they had to leave to bring her to the hospital. The police officer stood there quietly after that.

Our neighbor showed up at the side door, peering in with a panicked look. I knew her well. She and my mom were friends, and I would go over to her house whenever my mom wasn't home and I needed anything. She and the police officer spoke outside before he returned and told the firefighter, "She's got him when we leave."

As the chaos around me subsided, I finally started to calm down and was able to hang up the phone with the dispatcher. Before ending the call, she told me, "Great job, hon. You were very brave for your mom."

Right after that, the paramedics took my mom out to the ambulance.

Seeing her pass by got me scared again—the IV, blood spots on the sheet near her arm, oxygen mask, closed eyes, and the tears running down her face. She appeared limp, her body shifting around as the paramedics pushed the gurney. It was all new and frightening to me.

The firefighter held my hand and walked me out to the ambulance. He asked the paramedics to hold on for a second before they loaded her in the back. "Go give your mom a kiss before they go," he told me.

In the sunlight, I saw her skin color had changed. It looked like it had more life. I held her hand and kissed her on the forehead. She didn't open her eyes, but she squeezed my hand. I knew she was going to be okay.

The police car left first, then the ambulance, both with their lights and sirens running. The other firefighters were already getting back into the fire engine. It was time for the firefighter who had done so much for me to go. He glanced over at my neighbor, making sure she was still there. Before getting into the truck, he kneeled in front of me and said, "You saved your mom's life today." He stood up, put his hand on my shoulder, squeezed it, and said, "You are my hero."

He was there for me during the most stressful event of my life up to that point. He saw me and sensed the struggle I was facing. Instead of turning away and focusing solely on his responsibilities as a firefighter, he chose to take care of me, to make a connection that made all the difference in the world to me at that moment. Maybe he did that with every kid he met during responses, but that didn't matter to me. What mattered was that he cared about me that day. And it was that day that I decided I wanted a job in public service when I grew up that would allow me to help people the way he'd helped me.

The memory of the firefighter got me thinking about the connections I made on the trail too. The relationships with most of the hikers I met became strong very quickly, stronger than many I'd spent years building with people in my everyday life. We shared some of the most intimate

Five Million Steps **69**

details with each other, sometimes only minutes after meeting: successes, struggles, dreams, fears, traumas the trail was healing for us, and the things we were trying to discover during our journeys. No subject was off the table. We saw each other on our best days and our worst days. They poured into me, and I poured into them. They were fascinated by my life experiences, and I was fascinated by theirs. All with love, care, and respect for each other, free of judgment, and no image to uphold. We were all free to be our authentic selves.

Those strong connections were the result of how vulnerable we all were on the trail. We were equals, all walking on the same piece of trail, exposed to the same conditions, experiencing similar emotions, carrying everything we had on our backs, and sleeping on the ground in the woods. What we had and who we were at home didn't matter. What did matter, though, was that we had each other.

Like other times in my life, it was the people on the trail and moments we shared that were the most memorable and meaningful parts of the journey. It was similar to many of the connections I made throughout my military career. But the farther I got on the PCT, the more I realized how much I was missing toward the end of my career.

As I progressed through the ranks, took positions of increased responsibility, and led larger organizations, the deep connections I appreciated earlier in my career started to change. They no longer felt as genuine and seemed to be more transactional. I still had great connections with the people closest to me, but the connections I loved the most—the ones with young people at the beginning of their leadership journeys—became rarer.

My passion for taking care of people was still the same. My ability to make positive changes, influence other key decision makers, shape cultures, and create climates that allowed people to thrive all increased over time. But the opportunity to build meaningful connections, to get to know people on a personal level, to earn their trust, to watch them succeed, and to help them through difficult times all decreased. The more senior I got, the more I was surrounded by other senior leaders. There were hardly any younger people around.

I loved what I could do for people on a large scale, but I missed the face-to-face interaction and the real differences I could make in people's lives. Over seven years and six assignments, I went from being the senior enlisted leader of an organization of 95 people to one with over 122,000. I no longer had the time to build meaningful connections with many people. I traveled around the world and met with thousands of people, but I was in and out most of the time on short visits. Although I wanted it to be genuine, and I appreciated and cherished the time I had, it was nowhere near as satisfying as the connections that allowed me to be a part of their daily lives and see them grow over time, personally and professionally.

Although it was a privilege to serve in those positions, I wasn't as personally fulfilled. Connecting with people on the PCT—like the hiker who gave me my trail name, AYCE, the lady who tried to help me at the 7-Eleven in Big Bear Lake, Mary and Dan, as well as countless others I met throughout my hike—gave me the fulfillment I was missing. Those connections were the best part of the journey.

CHAPTER 8

# BADASS DAD

My alarm was set for 4:30 a.m., but I woke up fifteen minutes before it went off. Today was going to be a big day. I went to sleep excited, and the first thing my brain told me when I opened my eyes was *Get up; let's go!* It was as if I had blinked, and it was already morning. I'd camped five miles south of Forester Pass, the highest point on the Pacific Crest Trail at 13,200 feet above sea level. It's also the first major pass for northbound hikers. I had no "practice" passes before this one to gain some experience and calm my nerves.

I'd made camp at a small site next to a river at eleven thousand feet, and it was cold. The sun hadn't risen yet, but there was enough light to see my breath as I lay on my back and blew up toward the ceiling of my tent. A fine layer of frost sparkled on the walls from the condensation that had built up and frozen while I slept. I was excited to get moving, but I was not looking forward to the cold that would hit me as soon as I got out from under my warm quilt.

I'd drunk almost a liter of water before going to sleep to replenish what I had lost during my long day and in preparation for the tough climb ahead. Most of the water sources at higher elevations were still frozen and inaccessible. The river I was camped next to was reported to be the last reliable water source for ten miles, over and beyond Forester Pass, and I took advantage by drinking as much as my body could reasonably handle before starting my approach.

As soon as I started moving and the edges of my quilt lifted, I felt the familiar but unwelcome drafts entering. My body heat escaped, and I shivered as soon as that first chill hit me. The goose bumps rose, and my full bladder told me it was time to go.

Still hiding under my quilt, I quickly unzipped my tent door and reached for my socks, just outside. *Shit, they're frozen solid.* The temperature had dropped below freezing overnight, and they were frozen where I'd draped them over my shoes. As I had done every day before, I'd taken off my shoes and socks before getting into my tent. I set them under the vestibule to air out and let the sweat dry overnight. Not that night, though. The sweat didn't have a chance to evaporate before freezing.

My bladder warned me again, this time of an impending accident if I didn't get up and out of the tent to relieve myself, so I slid my warm, bare feet into my also-frozen shoes. It was an incredibly unpleasant experience, pushing the limits of my bladder even further and my morale even lower. With no time to tie the frozen laces, I stumbled to a nearby tree, shoes flopping loosely, almost coming off with each step, and relieved myself.

I dashed back to my tent when I was done, jumped back inside, and huddled under my still-warm quilt to get comfortable again. It was time to get moving, though. I'd seen no other hikers around when I was outside of my tent, which meant I had the rare opportunity to be the first hiker over the pass that day, and hopefully have some time there by myself. I wasn't going to let that opportunity pass me by. Wanting to get on the trail and warmed up, I got dressed, put on a dry pair of socks before slipping into my frozen shoes, and packed up camp quickly.

Moving slowly at first, my body still warming up, I noticed the trail

**74** Jason France

was different from what I had seen before. When the wet soil froze and expanded overnight, it raised the trail's surface about an inch. The frozen soil crunched under my feet with every step, leaving sunken footprints behind me. I warmed up quickly and was soon moving at a fast pace across a large snowfield in the valley below the pass. The sun was rising behind the surrounding mountains, silhouetting them, while rays of sunshine shot across the sky. The moisture of my breath collected and created patches of frost on the front of my shoulders. My hands and face stung from the cold, and I had to squint to keep my eyes from burning. I felt strong, though. I had hiked close to eight hundred miles at that point, slowly rising in elevation the entire time and my body getting better conditioned in the process. There were few times in my life when I'd felt as strong and confident as I did then. I was ready to get into the mountains.

My excitement and nervousness of entering the Sierra was still growing. I just needed to get this first pass knocked out to calm my nerves. I had heard stories about Forester's difficulty and watched videos documenting people's experiences with it as well. Now it was time for me to take it on, to be the first one over that day. There was no one ahead of me that I could watch, to see what route they took or if there were dangerous spots I would have to traverse, but my confidence still grew with every step.

I continued toward the base of the climb. I crossed more snow patches that covered the trail, seeing footprints left by other hikers, constantly scanning ahead for signs of the trail hidden beneath the snow. I mistakenly crossed a snow-covered frozen lake, only realizing I was no longer on the trail when I heard cracking noises beneath my feet. Adrenaline rushed through me from the initial fright before I hurried off the ice.

Then it was up the steep and rocky section of the trail that zigzagged up the mountain and to the pass. There were sheer ledges and loose rock the entire climb. It was exhilarating to hike on the edge of such big drop-offs, where the smallest mistake or misstep could have cost me my life.

Five Million Steps    **75**

As I made the final approach to the top, I looked back and saw three hikers about a mile behind me. *I'll have plenty of time to myself at the top!*

After two and a half hours of climbing, I reached the top of Forester Pass, breathing heavily and sweating despite the cold. I dropped my pack, and my breath was immediately taken away by the sharp sting of the wind hitting the back of my sweat-soaked shirt. Putting on my puffy jacket, I was warm again and enjoyed my time alone at the highest point on the PCT. It was a special moment for me, and worth every ounce of effort to get there. The views of the snowcapped mountains, perfectly clear skies, deep valleys carved into the granite, emerald-green and vibrant blue lakes, and the sun just peeking over the ridges to my east were all mine. I was the only one in the world with that view at that moment. It was the perfect reward for the accomplishment.

Even though I knew it wouldn't work, I still checked to see if I had cell service to make a FaceTime call to my family. It was the best way to share my world on the trail. I would flip the camera back and forth so they could see what I saw as I hiked. The excited look on their faces told me they were proud of me for what I was doing. It reminded me of the excitement on their faces after the many firsts they experienced when they were younger: riding a bike, doing a flip on a trampoline, flying down a snow-covered hill on a sled, and shooting down a giant waterslide. Those memories always bring a smile to my face.

Having no luck getting cell service, I took pictures and videos to capture the experience and then just sat there, leaning against a rock, resting and taking it all in, knowing I would have to continue soon. *This is badass. I wish Joseph and Justin were here with me to see this!* I took out a Snickers bar that I'd brought specifically for my celebration at the top.

It reminded me of hiking the Northern Loop Trail in Mount Rainier National Park with Joseph when he was twelve. It was his first big backpacking trip, forty miles over four days and three nights. It was a tough trail,

**76** Jason France

and sharing one of my biggest passions with my oldest son felt incredible. He was the youngest kid I saw on the trail. We got so many compliments from other hikers on how well he was doing and how surprising it was to see a kid his age on that trail. His confidence was through the roof, and I was beaming with pride the entire trip. I had hiked that same trail a few years earlier and knew which day would be the toughest, ending at Mystic Lake. I brought two Snickers bars and kept them hidden in my food bag, specifically to celebrate there. We set up camp, explored the area, swam in the lake, and got a tour of the remote ranger cabin from two rangers. The trip was full of proud-father moments, but that day was extra special. It was perfect, and we celebrated in camp at the end of the day with our Snickers bars.

That memory made me realize that this journey wasn't only for me. It was for my sons too. "Dad" is the best title I've ever held. The moment they came into my life, they gave me greater purpose and made me want to do better in all aspects of my life. I am so proud to be their father and proud of the great things they both do. Here was an opportunity to make them proud of me.

I grew up without a father. My mother was single for most of my child-hood. I never met my biological father; he and my mother divorced around the time I was born. She remarried shortly after that, but they divorced when I was in kindergarten, and I have no real memories of him. Despite a couple of boyfriends and a few acquaintances she had over the years while I was growing up, I never had a father figure or positive male role model to emulate. She married a third time when I was fifteen. He was only nine years older than me, and although we got along and he always treated me well, it never felt like a father-son relationship. And by that point, even though it may have been unfair to him, it was too late. I had been excited and then disappointed too many times to accept someone. I felt out of place most of the time they were together too, so I kept to myself as much as I

Five Million Steps    **77**

could the last few years I lived with them.

The best examples of being a father came from my father-in-law, both through stories my wife told me from when she grew up but mainly through the acceptance, care, and love he has always shown me. Their family had the structure and connection I wanted as a kid but never experienced, and they welcomed me as part of their family the first time we met.

Once Joseph came into our lives, everything was new to me. I was learning as I went, doing everything for the first time, hoping not to screw up too bad. I felt that learning how to be a good father was the most important thing for me to do in my life, and I wanted to get it right. But I had no idea what I was doing. I used what I wanted as a kid to shape my actions as a father. Not only was being a father new to me, but not knowing what I was doing was new to me too. I was the guy who always worked hard, learned, and tried to perfect everything in my life so I wouldn't fail. But the thing I needed to be the best at, out of anything else in my life, I had no clue about. It was scary as hell to me. What I did know was that I would always be there for my son and, later, my second son. Looking back, I believe I've learned just as much from them as they've learned from me.

I was almost thirty-three years old when Joseph was born and thirty-eight when Justin was born. I was nearly twenty years into my career. All the cool stuff that would be exciting to a kid—being a military working dog handler, shooting guns, jumping out of airplanes, driving cool vehicles—I did earlier in my career, or it was coming to an end as the air force put me on a different career path.

My sons knew what I did at work. They knew what I did was important. They knew I traveled a lot. They saw pictures and videos of me that I shared or were posted on social media. I knew they were proud of me, but it just wasn't the same. My jobs weren't that cool through the eyes of kids their age. I wanted to do something big; something they knew was awesome; something to earn the look of pride that, as a parent, is one of the most meaningful things in the world.

Two big moments stick out to me when I saw that pride in their eyes. For Joseph, it was in 2008. We were stationed at Moody Air Force Base in Valdosta, Georgia, one of my favorite assignments. I was on "jump status," where part of my job was parachuting from military aircraft.

Our training jumps were mainly at night and on drop zones in remote areas. But we would occasionally jump onto the runway on the base, sometimes during the day. The airfield would be closed to all aircraft except the ones we jumped from. Our families sometimes came to watch us too, and Monica and Joseph finally had the opportunity to come watch me. Jumping was one of the things I loved most about my job and a highlight of my career. Doing it in front of the people I loved made it even more meaningful.

On that particular day, we were jumping from a C-130 Hercules aircraft, and we were conducting "ramp jumps," where we would jump from the open ramp at the tail of the aircraft instead of the paratroop (side) doors. Ramp jumps were rare and very popular among parachutists. It was like jumping into a big movie screen.

I was the jumpmaster for the operation. My job was to ensure the safety of everyone on the jump that day, both on the ground and in the air. Being the jumpmaster also meant I would lead the team of paratroopers off the ramp and be the first person to jump from the aircraft.

As we prepared, I was focused on my responsibilities and didn't think much about my family being there to watch. We went through the long and detailed sequence of roll call for everyone jumping that day, an operations brief where we explained all the details about the jump, and rehearsals for everything we were going to do at every step of the operation. After that we went through the rigorous process of putting on and inspecting our parachutes and equipment, preparing and inspecting the aircraft we were jumping from, and more briefings with the paratroopers and aircrew before finally loading everyone on the aircraft and taking off.

Five Million Steps **79**

Once in the air, it was another thorough and detailed process to get everyone ready to jump. Twenty minutes away from the drop zone, I got the notification from the aircraft's loadmaster—the member of the aircrew that is responsible for, among many other things, safety, operating the systems on the aircraft, and communicating between the pilots and jumpmaster during flight—that we were approaching the drop zone. That was always an exciting moment, as it was time for me to get everyone ready to jump. I moved to the back of the airplane, near the closed ramp. Facing all the jumpers, I gave them the first time warning.

"TWENTY MINUTES," I yelled over the sound of the airplane's engines, simultaneously opening and closing both hands twice, giving them a visual signal of the number twenty. The jumpers all yelled back to me, "TWENTY MINUTES," letting me know they heard and were alert and ready to go. Every time warning and jump command I gave was echoed back to me as we prepared to jump.

The loadmaster gave me the second notification when we were ten minutes away from the drop zone. I hooked my static line to the anchor line cable, a strong cable that runs the length of the aircraft above our heads that all jumpers connect their static lines to. It's the anchor point for the static line that opens the parachutes after we jump out of the airplane.

"TEN MINUTES." I flashed another hand signal to the jumpers, and the aircrew turned on the "red lights." Everything moved quickly from that point.

"GET READY." I saw the anticipation and excitement on the jumpers' faces. They unbuckled their seat belts and got ready to stand.

"FIRST-PASS PERSONNEL, STAND UP." The jumpers all stood up from their seats, some moving around to adjust equipment and parts of their parachute harnesses that had moved during the flight while they were sitting. Their looks shifted from excitement to sharp focus. Their attention to detail was critical for the safety of themselves and their teammates.

"HOOK UP." They attached the snap hook on the end of their static lines to the anchor line cable.

"CHECK STATIC LINES." The jumpers checked their lines, ensuring their snap hook was properly attached to the anchor line cable and holding their lines in the position needed to jump safely out of the aircraft. They also checked the static line of the jumper in front of them, double checking to ensure the line was not mistakenly wrapped around their arms or equipment, potentially injuring them as they exited. The jumpmaster safety, an additional jumpmaster on board and the jumpmaster's second set of eyes, also inspected the jumpers' static lines, a third check to ensure everyone's safety.

"CHECK EQUIPMENT." Each jumper went through the standard sequence of checking their helmet and parts of their parachute harnesses to ensure nothing had moved or detached during the flight.

"SOUND OFF FOR EQUIPMENT CHECK." One at a time, from the back of the line toward me, each jumper tapped the jumper in front of them on the butt with their left hand, yelling, "OKAY." The process continued until the first jumper in the line, who stood facing me, put his hand in front of my face and yelled, "ALL OKAY, JUMPMASTER." I slapped his hand in acknowledgment.

Six minutes from the drop zone, the aircraft slowed to 130 knots (about 150 miles per hour), and the loadmaster opened the ramp. That was always one of the most exciting parts of the jump for me: watching the door open slowly, squinting as my eyes adjusted to the bright light, feeling the rush of cool air entering the plane, and seeing everything outside and below us—the houses, cars, and people—looking so small. The loadmaster completed his inspection of the ramp, then turned to me. He pointed his open hand toward the edge and yelled, "AIR FORCE, YOUR DOOR." I gave him a thumbs-up.

It was time for my initial outside air safety check. The loadmaster, secured to the aircraft with a harness and line so he couldn't fall out, walked with me toward the hinge of the open ramp. I got down on one knee and

Five Million Steps **81**

stuck my head outside to look toward the ground and behind the aircraft, making sure there was nothing near us in the air or on the ground that could be dangerous for us when we jumped out. It was clear.

It was always a rush for me to do that, essentially hanging my head out the side of an airplane with a huge smile on my face, getting blasted by the wind, over a thousand feet above the ground. I pulled my head back inside, stayed on one knee, and kept watch on the jumpers and crew to make sure everything was still good to go.

One minute away from the drop zone, I gave the next time warning to the jumpers: "ONE MINUTE" as I signaled to them with my index finger pointing up. *Almost time!*

Thirty seconds out, I gave my last time warning and hand signal—"THIRTY SECONDS"—and conducted one more outside air check, sticking my head back outside and looking down and behind the aircraft again to make a final check for hazards. *All good.* As I stood back up, I adjusted my grip on my static line, repositioned myself in front of the jumpers, then turned and walked toward the edge of the open ramp. The other jumpers slowly took their places behind me. I stopped a couple of feet away from the edge and focused my gaze on the jump caution lights.

"STAND BY," I shouted, letting the jumpers know we were seconds away from exiting the aircraft. Finally, I raised my left hand with my elbow bent at a ninety-degree angle, ready to signal them to go.

Seconds later, the "red light" turned to green. I gave my final command of "FOLLOW ME" and waved my left hand forward. Then I walked off the end of the ramp, leading the rest of the jumpers out and into the air.

Stepping off the ramp, I got into a tight body position, hands on my reserve parachute in case I had to use it, and bending slightly forward so I could see the ground below. All this before catching the wind, getting tossed around, and the feeling of falling caught me in the gut. I loved that feeling. It never got old. I also started the count that would let me know

**82** Jason France

if my main parachute failed to open and I needed to activate my reserve.

"ONE THOUSAND, TWO THOUSAND, THREE THOUSAND, FOUR THOUSAND . . . OOOF." I exhaled sharply as the opening shock of my parachute deploying hit me. Sometimes it's quite a shock to your body when your parachute opens and you decelerate from 130 knots to less than 10 in about four seconds, especially if you don't maintain the right body position.

After getting tossed around and swinging back and forth for a few seconds, I looked up and checked my parachute. *It's fully open, no malfunctions, no damage. Grab the toggles, 360-degree check complete, no twists in my risers or suspension lines, and I'm not descending quicker than I should be. All good!*

All the other jumpers had exited the aircraft, were under good chutes, and had good spacing between each other. We were using MC1-1D parachutes that day. They are thirty-five feet in diameter, and the rate of descent is about twenty feet per second. We jumped from 1,250 feet, so it would only take about a minute to reach the ground.

I continued to look around, maintaining my bearings, and searched for a place to land. Looking behind me, I saw my wife's SUV parked just outside the edge of the drop zone. I saw her and Joseph sitting in front of her vehicle. It was a rare opportunity, the only time in my career when my wife and son had come out to watch me jump, and I couldn't resist making it a memorable experience for us all. I immediately turned toward them and tried to get as close as possible before landing.

Technically, I should have stayed with my group, but I knew the area directly in front of my family was still inside the designated drop zone. I also knew I wouldn't break any safety rules or put anyone at risk by landing there. So I pulled down hard on my left toggle, turned 180 degrees, and descended toward them.

At that point, I had been jumping for eight years and was confident in my ability to maneuver and land exactly where I wanted to, so it was time for me to show off a little bit. As you descend, you are supposed to maneuver your parachute to face into the wind to offset the forward thrust that the parachute creates. "Running with the wind" is when you do the opposite. The wind will be at your back, your speed will increase, and you'll likely go too fast to land safely. However, with experience, you can run with the wind to quickly get across the drop zone, turn at the right moment, and decrease your speed to a safe level before you land. I did exactly that and landed just a few yards away from my wife and son. Joseph was jumping up and down excitedly as I approached and landed.

After removing my parachute harness, I stood and looked at them. Joseph's giant grin and the wave of his little hand are things I will never forget. He'd just watched his dad jump from a military airplane, parachute down with a bunch of other paratroopers, and land right in front of him and his mom. That was a badass-dad moment.

For Justin it was during a white water rafting trip in Colorado.

I went white water rafting for the first time when I was eleven years old. It was on the Truckee River in California during the summer between fifth and sixth grades. My experience that day was foundational. It was the first time I felt the thrill of danger and excitement. I remember the rush of the wind in my ears, seeing flashes of the water, the rocks, and the sky as we were tossed around, and hearing the screams and laughs of our group.

After we "survived" and were back on shore, my legs and arms were cold, shaking, and exhausted from the work I'd put in. For the first time, I had that sensation in my gut: the butterflies. I knew right away that I was hooked. I was an instant adrenaline junkie, and I wanted that feeling again. That experience on the river led me to all the other things I've done in my life to get a feeling like that first one: skateboarding, skiing, mountain biking, scuba diving, bungee jumping, parachuting, rappelling off buildings and cliffs and from helicopters, shooting guns, and "playing" with explosives.

My opportunity to share that foundational experience finally came when Justin, Joseph, and I went on a five-day trip to Colorado to enjoy some outdoor adventures. Our best day was when we took a white water rafting trip down Clear Creek near Idaho Springs, Colorado. My sons were excited to try something new, and I was thrilled to share an experience similar to the one that was so meaningful to me when I was around their age.

I did most of the talking as we drove to the guide company the morning of our trip. They were both quiet, and I could sense their anticipation and a bit of nervousness growing. When we arrived, we met our guide and started the process of signing waivers, meeting the people we would be rafting with, receiving safety briefs, and putting on our wet suits, helmets, and flotation devices. As my sons became more familiar with their equipment and met the people we would share the ride with, their nerves subsided and their excitement grew. The serious looks turned into smiles, and the quietness turned into laughter. They were still sharply focused, though, paying close attention to everything our guide shared; I was proud to see that.

We rode in the guide company's vans to the river. During the drive, as we got closer to our put-in—the point where our trip would start—we could see the river from the highway. My sons' eyes were fixed on the churning water, the cliffs and rocks surrounding the river, and the other rafts passing through where we would soon be. Their smiles grew, but they also seemed to realize that this would be tough. This was no smooth and easy float down the river. Seeing their excitement and adventurous spirit as they faced a new, potentially dangerous challenge was another proud-dad moment for me.

Arriving at the put-in spot, the preparation process continued. Once the rafts were unloaded, we had our safety and emergency procedure briefings. The guide assigned our positions and duties. While still on shore, we practiced communicating, paddling, and working together as we would on the water.

I was in the front left position, Justin was directly behind me, and Joseph was the second person on the right side—right behind me and to

Five Million Steps **85**

my right, directly across from Justin. After a few last-minute checks and reminders, we pushed off from the shore and were on our way down the river. Glancing back at my sons, I was brought back to my trip on the Truckee River. I saw my younger self in both of them for that brief moment: Justin's bright-yellow helmet cocked to one side, eyes peeking up at me from under the brim; Joseph's red flotation vest, straps tightened all the way but still loose on his thin frame; both grinning ear to ear. It was a moment I wish I could hold on to forever.

The river was tame at first, and our guide talked us through as we practiced paddling, reading and navigating obstacles, and working together as a crew. He showed us examples of all the new rafting terms we had learned: eddies, boils, chutes, holes, channels, and sleepers, all while keeping us working together and improving our skills.

Finally, the real fun started as we rounded a bend in the river. I looked back at Justin and Joseph, whose eyes and smiles were huge, and said, "Here we go, guys. This is it!"

We were fully immersed in our white water rafting experience for the next hour. The sound of the powerful rushing river, the walls of water that hit us as our raft bounced up and down in the waves, the flashes I got of my sons' intense looks of concentration and focus, and the cheers when we made it through each scary stretch.

We had a group of smaller people in our boat. I just happened to be the strongest person in our group, so the guide and I worked together to navigate the more difficult areas. He yelled, "Forward paddle, front left! Dig! You've gotta pull us through!" a few times that day.

The most exciting moment was when the front of our raft dipped into a hole, popped back up quickly, and tossed Justin into the air. In my peripheral vision, I saw his right foot and hand in the air behind me, almost above my head. Joseph reached over, grabbed his leg, and pulled him back down onto his seat, like nothing had happened. More cheers came from the others on the raft, and my sons laughed and screamed.

Our excitement subsided as we approached the end of our trip and prepared to reach the shore. We were all tired from the work but exhilarated from the experience.

Just before our raft touched the shore, the guide said, "Thanks for carrying us today, front left. You're the man!"

Before I could respond, Justin shouted, "That's my dad! He's strong!"

When I looked back at him, he had that smile and look I live for in his eyes. The way he looked at me in those few seconds deeply touched my heart.

Through the eyes of my nine-year-old son, part of what we had just experienced was frightening, probably some of the most intense moments of his life up to that point. But he faced everything the river threw at him head-on, and I was so proud of him. And what touched my heart even more was that, in his view, his dad was the one who saved the day.

Both events I described lasted only a few seconds. I spent years hoping to get those smiles and see those looks in their eyes again. I thought hiking the PCT might give me that again, and the experiences I shared with them on my journey did just that.

But most importantly, I wanted my PCT journey to encourage them to dream big, keep those dreams alive, and turn them into reality. I hoped to inspire them to pursue their passions and find fulfillment. To challenge themselves, do hard things, and understand that character is forged, and the greatest rewards are often earned by pushing through obstacles, overcoming hard times and self-doubt, and growing from failures. I wanted them to see how important it is to slow down, be still sometimes, and enjoy the moments because those are the best parts of any journey. And that sometimes we need to disconnect from what consumes us in our everyday lives and appreciate the things around us that we are often too distracted to see.

And I wanted to teach them that you're never too old to do badass stuff!

CHAPTER 9

# IN THE MOMENT

My summit of Forester Pass was one of my most memorable moments on the PCT. The tough climb, being the first one to the summit that day and having it all to myself, the stunning views of the surrounding mountains, valleys, and lakes in every direction. I was completely immersed in the experience and fully present for myself. It was perfect.

Shortly after beginning my descent from the pass, though, my mind slipped back into planning mode, and my perfect moment completely left my thoughts. I'm a planner by nature. I have been for as long as I can remember. And I've become good at it over the years. I was hopeful that my experience on the PCT would break me away from my habit of having to plan—and often overplan—just about every aspect of my life. But sometimes old habits die hard.

I had hiked five miles from my previous night's camp to the pass, and I had eighteen miles left to make it to the trailhead. From there I was going to hitchhike into the town of Bishop for a much-needed zero-day. The eighty miles from Kennedy Meadows to Forester Pass had been tough. It was my first section in the Sierra, and the steep climbs and descents were completely different from what I had navigated in the desert section, where the terrain was much more forgiving. Despite enjoying everything the mountains were giving me, I was worn out and ready to get into town to rest and recharge before heading into the next mountain stretch.

My planning for this last stretch was as perfect as it could be. I was on target with my daily mileage projections, my pace and time estimates were sharp, and my food planning was so accurate that I would end the four-day, eighty-mile stretch with only an almond butter packet, three instant coffee packets, and two packets of electrolyte drink mix. I was proud of myself and ready to geek out on my next plan: getting into Bishop.

Here's what was going through my mind as I descended from Forester Pass:

*Okay, it's eight o'clock and Forester is done. About eight miles to the trail junction to Kearsarge Pass. Should take me about four hours with the big ups and downs.*

*Off the PCT and onto the Kearsarge Pass Trail. Three miles to Kearsarge from there. Big climb, so I'll say ninety minutes to the top of the pass.*

*Four and a half miles down to the trailhead and parking lot at Onion Valley. All downhill, pack is light—less than two hours to knock that out. Should get there between three thirty and four. Guthook comments say it's a super easy hitch, tons of people coming off the trail at that time. A lot of them head to Bishop, biggest town in the area. The ride to Bishop is fifty-five miles, a little over an hour.*

*Check into the hotel by five. Plug in my electronics to charge. Lay out all my gear to air out. Shower. Town clothes. Fifteen-minute walk to the laundromat. They close at ten. Plenty of time. Start my clothes and hit the Mexican restaurant across the street. Tacos and a beer. Line up my morning ride while I eat.*

*Back to the laundromat. Clothes into the dryer and hit the frozen yogurt place I heard about from five hikers. Frozen yogurt and wine. I don't even like wine, but hell yeah.*

*Back to the laundromat to pick up my clothes. Fifteen minutes back to the hotel to drop off my clothes. Probably around eight by now.*

*Hit the grocery store across the street. They close at eleven. Plenty of time. Six-day resupply for 120 miles to Mammoth Lakes.*

*Back to the room. Check my gear. Pack everything up. In bed by ten. Up at six. Breakfast in the room. Check out.*

*Ride picks me up at seven. On the trail by eight thirty. Up and over Kearsarge Pass, and back on the PCT by one.*

*Awesome plan, Jay.*

*Move out.*

My plan was going great . . . until it wasn't. The fifty-five hundred feet of climbing and six thousand feet of descents over the twenty-three miles that day slowed me down more than I thought it would. I underestimated the climb over Kearsarge Pass and found it more difficult than Forester, even though it's about fifteen hundred feet lower in elevation. I was pushing so hard to get to the trailhead that I hardly noticed any of the beautiful views I was speeding past. The trail was packed with day hikers too. I hiked past all of them, not wanting to talk to anyone, still focused on getting off the trail. I only stopped to talk once, to an older couple from France. It looked like the wife was having some health issues, so I stopped to see if she was okay. After I learned she was, the three of us talked for quite a while before I realized it was already past four o'clock and I still had two more miles to go to reach the parking lot. We said our goodbyes, and I jogged the last two miles to the parking lot at the trailhead. It was approaching five when I finally arrived.

What I found at Onion Valley was a near-empty parking lot, exactly the opposite of what I had read in the Guthook comments. I looked back up toward the trail I had just come down and scanned the few trails that branched out and went up the surrounding mountains, but I saw no one. I checked to see if I had cell reception so I could try to contact any of the local trail angels who were offering rides—nothing. My plan was falling apart.

Six o'clock came and went, and still no one was coming down or leaving the parking lot. I walked through the small campground near the trailhead and asked five different people if they could give me a ride into Bishop, and even offered to pay them, but no luck. So back to the parking lot I went to try my luck again.

As I came out of the campground and into the trailhead parking lot, I saw two hikers coming down the trail, just a short distance from the trailhead sign. As they got closer, I saw that it was the French couple, Gabriel and Valerie.

"Hey, guys!" I said with a wave and a smile. "How was the rest of your hike?"

"Hello again, my friend," Gabriel said with a big grin. "It was beautiful. Thank you for asking. I'm surprised to see you here. I thought you would have left by now."

"No cars have left. I think all the cars here belong to people camping on the trail tonight."

Valerie piped up quickly. "We can take you to Independence! Isn't that where you said you were going?"

The small town of Independence is about halfway to Bishop. "I'm trying to get to Bishop, actually, but a ride to Independence would be awesome. I should be able to catch a ride to Bishop from there."

We loaded into their SUV and were soon on our way down the winding road to Independence. We spent the thirty-minute drive talking about their travel adventures. I was focused on adjusting my plan in my head, though, and didn't contribute much to the conversation. It was almost eight o'clock when they dropped me off. We said our farewells, and I thanked Gabriel and Valerie for their generosity.

I was now at a gas station in the middle of town, next to US 395, the four-lane highway that leads directly to Bishop. The road was still busy with cars, trucks pulling recreational vehicles, and semitrucks hauling freight. *This should be too easy*, I thought, standing next to the highway with my thumb out.

I stood there for close to an hour without even a glance from anyone passing by. Finally, a hiker staying in a hotel across the street noticed me and yelled, "Hey, bro! Do you need phone numbers for a ride? I've got three numbers for locals giving rides to hikers!"

I'd been so focused on getting a hitch that I failed to realize I had cell reception and could call someone for a ride. "That would be awesome, man! I'm trying to get to Bishop tonight," I yelled back.

He grabbed the list from his room, ran across the highway, and handed me the wrinkled piece of paper with three names and phone numbers scribbled on it. "Here you go, man. It's pretty late, so I doubt any of them are still running. If you can't land a ride, come knock on room 112. You can crash on the floor. I'm with three other hikers, but we'll make room for you. All the hotels here are full."

"I really appreciate this, man. Thanks so much."

"Anytime, bro. Good luck!"

Still standing on the side of the highway, I dialed the first number. No answer. Same with the second number. *Last chance, please freakin' answer!* I dialed the last number. No answer. *Shit! I'm screwed.* It was almost nine o'clock, and I was stuck in a small town that didn't have anything I needed. No grocery store for the six-day resupply I had to buy—only a gas station convenience store with snacks. There were no rooms available, and I didn't want to pile into a room with four other hikers I didn't know. The restaurants were all closed. There was no laundromat. It was official at that point: my plan had completely fallen apart.

My phone buzzed in my pocket. It was the last number I'd dialed calling me back.

"Hello!" I answered.

Five Million Steps **93**

"Yeah. This is Derek. I got a missed call from this number."

"Hey, Derek. My name is Jay. Thanks for calling me back. I'm a PCT hiker looking for a ride to Bishop. I'm in Independence at the Valero station. I know it's late, but would it be possible to get a ride tonight?"

"You're in luck. I'm about to pass through Independence, heading back to Bishop. I just dropped off some hikers at Onion Valley that are camping there tonight and getting back on the trail in the morning. I just got back in cell range and saw your missed call."

"You're a lifesaver, Derek. Thanks."

"You're welcome. Just hang out there. I'll be there in about ten minutes."

I grabbed some snacks and a Dr Pepper for the road, and like clockwork, Derek was there in exactly ten minutes. Finally, I was on my way to Bishop, forty miles away. Derek filled the drive with great stories about the hikers he had met over the ten years he'd been giving rides in the area. He was full of stories and facts about the area's history too. He shared one of the most interesting ones after we pulled out of the gas station and passed the Inyo County Courthouse. That was where Charles Manson had his preliminary hearing in 1969 on charges for possessing stolen property, part of the series of events that led to his indictment for the Tate–LaBianca murders.

I was glad Derek talked most of the way to Bishop. I wasn't in the mood to talk much myself. I was still frustrated about my plan failing and being so far off schedule. I was exhausted too. Pushing hard all day on a tough section of trail had worn me out.

We finally got to Bishop just before eleven o'clock. Derek dropped me off at the Motel 6. He had brought a group of hikers there that afternoon and thought they probably still had rooms available. Thankfully, they did. I booked a room for three nights instead of only two. The pressure I had put on myself physically and mentally in the last stretch had caught up to me, and I wanted two full days off the trail to recover. Derek stuck around to make sure I got a room and offered to give me a ride back to Onion Valley after my zero-days. I took him up on the offer and thanked him again for his help before he drove off.

As soon as I got to my room, I dropped my pack in the corner. I had no interest in anything but taking a shower and getting some sleep. *I'll deal with all that crap tomorrow. What a freakin' day.* After one of the quickest showers ever, I was in bed and knocked out as soon as my head hit the pillow.

My double-zero in Bishop was exactly what I needed. Two full days with no rushing and no pressure to get things done. Not only did I get the rest I needed and accomplished all the normal zero-day tasks, but the slower pace allowed me to reflect on a mistake I had been making far too often throughout my journey. I was missing some of the most important parts of the experience: the small moments. My push to get into Bishop was one of the biggest examples.

I'd allowed myself to become consumed by my plan. I'd rushed through the whole day, focusing on getting into Bishop and all the things I had to do when I got there while neglecting the things right in front of me the whole way. I had spent almost an entire day on the PCT, hiking through one of the most stunning areas in the country, fulfilling a childhood dream, and I'd done it with my eyes down and my legs carrying me as quickly as they could to get off the trail. In my haste, I had undoubtedly missed opportunities to meet some great people, passed tons of amazing views, and prevented any chance of being present for myself. I missed countless moments. Those moments are forever lost.

Three days later, I arrived at the trailhead much later than expected, in the early afternoon. Derek had been delayed that morning, so I'd checked out of my hotel, walked with my pack to a popular restaurant in town, and enjoyed a long, relaxing breakfast while I waited for him. We had two other hikers with us for the drive to Onion Valley and had a blast sharing stories and laughs the entire way. I completely lost track of time, and the drive seemed to fly by.

My pack was heavy with the six days' worth of food I needed for the 120-mile stretch to Mammoth Lakes. It was the heaviest food carry I had to make so far, making my climb back to Kearsarge Pass slow and difficult. I had just under eight miles of hiking before my trail intersected back with the PCT, but I was in no rush. I wasn't even sure how far I would go or where I would camp that night. The weather was perfect, clear skies and bright sun, but with a nice breeze to help tame the heat. My slow pace allowed me to take in all the amazing sights I had missed when I first hiked that section of trail three days ago. It was a completely different, and much better, experience.

I tried to be more in the moment and not plan every little detail of my trip. It wasn't easy, and I knew it would take a lot of focus and intentionality. Still, the shift in mindset gave me almost immediate results and led me to yet another incredibly memorable moment on my journey.

I took a long break at a beautiful spot, less than a mile from the PCT intersection. It was on a rock ledge facing south, with spectacular views of the Sierra in front of me and Bullfrog Lake below, surrounded by trees. The water was perfectly still, and the reflection of the mountains and sky on its surface showed the vibrant colors the sunset had cast. I was at the perfect spot, at the perfect moment, to take it all in.

I was running out of daylight, so I returned to the trail and continued my slow pace toward the PCT. My thoughts were still on the spot I had just left, though. And in what was probably the first truly spontaneous act of my journey, I turned back. *That spot is too good to pass up. I'm staying there tonight.* It was one of the best decisions I'd made in a long time.

I set up quickly, cowboy camping with a groundsheet, my sleeping pad, and quilt—no tent. I had a clear view of the sky, caught a perfect sunset, and watched the beautiful colors fade below the horizon as I dozed off. I woke up in the middle of the night to stars that seemed close enough to touch. There was no moon, so the sky was completely black, making the stars seem to shine brighter than ever. And I woke up to yet another amazing view: the sun rising over the Sierra.

I had lost track of the date, but glancing at my watch as the water for my coffee started to boil, I realized that it was the twentieth anniversary of my grandmother's passing, making the moment even more special. I got to share a beautiful moment and a cup of coffee with the woman who meant so much to me and was the first person to encourage me to hike the PCT.

CHAPTER 10

# SIMPLICITY

I had just finished a swim at Fisher Lake when I noticed a group of three hikers coming up the trail toward the lake. It was almost 5:00 p.m., and I had hiked only fourteen miles since a trail angel dropped me back off at the Etna Summit trailhead late that morning after a zero-day in Etna, California. I was trapped in yet another heat wave that seemed to have been following me for three weeks, and a dip in the cold water was exactly what I needed to recharge before heading on to my camp for the night.

I was fast approaching the border of California and Oregon, the next big milestone in my journey. I had reached the sixteen-hundred-mile point shortly after starting that morning, leaving less than a hundred miles until the border. It had been a long three months in the same state, and I was ready to leave California behind me.

I decided to have dinner at the lake to finish drying off and enjoy being near the water for a bit longer. I watched the three hikers walk up to the shore right next to me as I took my stove and food bag out of my pack. I could see they were worn out. The first guy, who was the tallest of the group, threw off his pack and plopped onto the ground before rolling onto his side, red-faced and panting. The other two—one with a bright-red buzz cut, the other with pineapple-print shorts—walked in circles with their arms above their heads, trying to catch their breath. The redhead shouted, "Fuuuuuck, that was an ass kicker!"

They had come from the same trailhead I had, and I recognized them from Etna. We'd eaten in the same restaurant the night before but didn't meet. Their packs were heavy; I watched the effort it took for the two standing to swing them off their shoulders and set them on the ground. All of their packs were big, about sixty liters each.

"What's up, guys? Long day?" I asked as I connected the gas canister to my stove.

"Yeah, man, today was an ass kicker," the redhead said again.

"You staying here tonight too?" the guy with the pineapple shorts asked.

"Nope, just going to have dinner here. I'm going to knock out a few more miles."

"How much farther are you going?" the pineapple guy asked.

"Not sure yet. I want to hit the border in three days, and if I push it, I can get into Seiad Valley tomorrow night."

"You're hiking the PCT?"

"Yeah."

"With that?" the tall guy yelled, still panting on the ground as he pointed at my pack with a look of surprise.

"Yeah. Why?"

"I just don't see how you can fit everything you need in a pack that small. You must love suffering."

It wasn't the first time I had heard comments like that. After all, my pack was, in fact, much smaller than what most other PCT hikers were hauling—only thirty-five liters. But I wasn't suffering at all. Quite the contrary. I was thriving. Over my decades of hiking, I had learned to appreciate a simple approach and carry only what I truly needed. That usually meant a much smaller and lighter pack than what most other hikers carried. I was long past the common backpacking term "you pack your fears." It wasn't a contest, though, as many hikers believed. I wasn't trying to impress or outdo anyone. My setup worked for me, and that's all I cared about.

"I get it, man," I said with a big smile. "It might not be for everyone, but it works for me. I'm not suffering at all." I couldn't ignore the fact that we'd all covered the same distance that day, but while I had plenty of energy left for the miles I was still to hike, they were all wiped out and done for the day.

The guy with the pineapple shorts chimed in again. "He's just jealous, bro. His shit weighs like sixty pounds. How much does your pack weigh, anyway?"

"Probably about twenty-five pounds."

"No fucking way!"

The next thirty minutes were spent answering questions about my gear, daily routine, daily mileage, and resupply strategy as I ate my dinner and prepared to get back on the trail. Like I had heard many comments about my pack size and my "suffering," I also spent a lot of time answering questions from those same people once they figured out that maybe I was on to something.

"Take care, gents," I said as I easily lifted my small pack onto my back. "Have a great night. I'll see you down the trail."

Back on the trail, putting more miles behind me but still not knowing where I would end for the day, my thoughts were on how simple but fulfilling my experience on the PCT had been so far. It was much more than just my small pack and the thirty-four items inside it. It was about the freedom I had because of my approach to everything on the trail: keep it simple; don't allow it to get complicated.

My days were as simple as they could be. I woke up when I wanted, lay in my tent as long as I wanted, took as long as I wanted to have my coffee and breakfast, and left camp and started hiking when I wanted. And then I walked, as long as I wanted, until I chose to stop. I took breaks whenever,

Five Million Steps **101**

wherever, and for as long as I wished. I even took naps in the middle of the day sometimes. If I wanted to spend an hour taking in a view, checking out wildlife, swimming in a remote lake, or talking with other hikers, I did. And when I got everything I wanted out of my day, I stopped and camped. Every day was new; sometimes the flow was similar to other days, sometimes completely different. It was all up to me, though, and I kept it as simple as possible.

That wasn't always my approach, though. I had evolved. I was once the hiker who had way too much and was, in fact, suffering. My first big hiking trip was on the Wonderland Trail in 2003. It's 93 miles long and circumnavigates Mount Rainier in Washington. I carried a 110-liter expedition pack and filled every bit of space with stuff, most of which I didn't even use and certainly didn't need. I overcomplicated everything on that trip: the plan, my gear, and my routine. I felt rushed, was constantly worn out from carrying so much, didn't take breaks, and didn't stop to admire the beauty around me. I finished the trail, but I didn't enjoy it as much as I could have.

Now, simplicity means efficiency, greater enjoyment, less frustration, less mental clutter, and greater fulfillment. If something doesn't add value, or if it takes away from the experience, I let it go. It goes far beyond my hiking experiences and applies to many other areas of my life—possessions, thoughts, and relationships, to name a few.

My late uncle Dennis was one of the first people in my life who showed me the importance of simplicity. He was one of the kindest and happiest people I've ever known. He was that cool uncle you always wanted to be around, a perpetual optimist who always saw the good in people and situations. He had a smile that would light up any room, he had an infectious laugh that would immediately cheer you up if you were feeling down, and he gave the best hugs. His off-the-wall style and appearance, always with mismatched clothes and big, messy hair, completed the whole package. There was no one like my Uncle Dennis.

I would listen for hours to the stories he told of his adventures, traveling to exciting places and meeting interesting people along the way. I don't think he ever held a full-time job. He worked to support his passions and simple lifestyle, bouncing from one job to another, making what he needed for the next adventure, the next dream. My Uncle Dennis did it all while living in his Volkswagen van with his best friend, a border collie named Zak. He was living the dream of modern-day van life before van life was even a thing.

As a young kid, I had a difficult time understanding his vagabond lifestyle. We moved a lot because we had to, not because we wanted to—ten times before I graduated high school and joined the air force. Dennis moved around by choice. We had very little, and life always seemed to be difficult. Dennis had very little but always seemed content.

I would ask him questions, like "Where is your house?" and "Where is your stuff?" His response was usually something like, "My van is my house, and I have everything I need." One of the most profound things he said about possessions was "Who needs stuff when I have you to make me happy?" I didn't understand what he meant until much later in life—unfortunately, after he was gone.

Throughout my entire childhood, I always thought I needed material things to be happy. I grew up thinking that a big, expensive house full of lots of expensive things and expensive cars in the driveway were what people were supposed to have. In my mind, that was what success looked like. It seemed to me that the people I saw who had those things were happy. It didn't make sense to me that someone with so little, like Dennis, could be so happy. Without me realizing it, he taught me valuable life lessons through the example he set by living a simple and happy life.

I approached camp eight miles after leaving Fisher Lake, still reflecting on how simplicity made my PCT journey so meaningful. There was a value in having only what was truly necessary; it made me appreciate the things I did have even more. And it reinforced what I already knew but sometimes lost sight of: that the simple things can bring you the most happiness.

Those simple things for me on the PCT were beautiful mountain views, the colorful skies of sunrises and sunsets, the smell of the forest after it rained, the butterflies that reminded me of my wife, the sound of the wind in the trees, waking up in the middle of the night to a sky full of bright stars, warm sun touching my face on a cold morning, eating ripe huckleberries on the side of the trail, and the moments with wonderful people whom I shared my journey with.

All those things were simple. All those things were free. And all those things created the best memories for me.

CHAPTER 11

# INTO THE DARKNESS

My family and I spent five days together in South Lake Tahoe, California. It was over Independence Day weekend, and the city was packed with tourists and holiday events. It felt nice to be a tourist, too, instead of a hiker for a few days, and our time together was filled with activities. We got everything we could out of it. Monica and I celebrated our wedding anniversary, which we had been apart for two weeks earlier. We enjoyed a private yoga session for our family on the shore of the lake, and we went to a magic show, hit the best restaurants, and enjoyed our time together as a family.

We had been planning our time there for months. The original plan was for them to fly into Reno, Nevada, grab a rental car, and pick me up from wherever I was on the trail. As the time got closer, though, I decided to surprise them by meeting them at the airport when they arrived. Not only did I think it would be fun to surprise them, but it would give us more time together since they wouldn't have to spend a large portion of a day finding and picking me up.

I wanted to get as many miles in as I could before meeting them so I could still finish the trail inside the window I was considering: long before

**105**

the first snowfall in the Cascades. To make it all happen, I hiked as fast as possible in the weeks leading up to their arrival, pushing the hardest in the final days. I was flying and made it to Donner Pass, sixty miles past my target of South Lake Tahoe.

I arrived at the pass exhausted and hungry. I had heard that the restaurant at Donner Ski Ranch gave a free beer to PCT hikers, so I stopped there for a meal, my free beer, and to figure out how I was going to get to the airport in Reno to meet up with my family in two days. The airport in Reno was about fifty-five miles away. There were no taxis or ride services available near Donner Pass. And hitching would be difficult due to the remoteness of the roads immediately around the pass and the fact that the main route to the airport, once out of the remote area, was Interstate 80, where hitchhiking is prohibited.

A young couple who had just finished a day hike in the area arrived at the restaurant when I did. They saw me drop my pack on the patio before entering and came over to me after I placed my order at the counter.

The man said, "Hey! I'm Kevin, and this is my wife, Nikki. Looks like you're hiking the PCT, something we hope to do someday too. Do you mind if we join you for lunch?"

I could tell immediately they were friendly people and told Kevin, "That would be great! I've been hiking solo for a while and would love some company."

As we ate, we told hiking stories and talked about our adventures, and I answered their questions about the PCT. Before I knew it, we had spent an hour and a half together, and it was time for me to figure out how I would get to Reno.

"This has been awesome, guys. Thanks for saying hello and spending some time with me," I said, standing up slowly as the tightness in my legs hit me. "Time for me to get moving now so I can get to Reno."

"What are you headed to Reno for?" Nikki asked.

"I'm spending five days off-trail with my family in Tahoe," I said. I also told them about my plan to surprise them at the airport. "Now I just need to figure out how to get there."

"We're from Reno!" Kevin said, smiling. "We'd be happy to give you a ride to the airport."

There's a saying in the hiking community, "The trail will provide," and that was one of the best examples of it I experienced on the trail. It was an incredible load off my mind.

We had fun on the drive to Reno too. I answered more questions about my other hiking experiences and my journey on the PCT. They shared more stories of their adventures: hiking, snowboarding, and traveling the world. They were such a fantastic couple. Before I knew it, we were at the airport, and after a quick thank-you and farewell, I picked up a rental car and went to a nearby hotel for a much-needed shower and some rest.

The next day was filled with the same zero-day routine as most other places despite having to do a little more than usual. I had to shop for, assemble, and mail the six resupply boxes that would take me through the rest of California and to my first stop in Oregon, just across the border. I was excited to see my family the next morning, and the day seemed to drag on.

I kept my inReach with me and responded to messages from Monica all day. To keep the surprise, I had to send her messages from it instead of my phone, just as I did when I was hiking. I also turned off the feature that sent a link to my location with each message so she couldn't see where I was: in downtown Reno. My plan worked, and I got everything done that would have taken a day away from our time together.

The following day at the airport, I hid behind a row of slot machines in the corridor outside the arrival gates. Peering over the top of the machines, I saw them come around the corner among the crowd of other passengers. I stepped out from behind the slot machines, holding a sign I had made with "Adventure dude looking for his family" written on it.

All three of them froze for a second, eyes wide open, heads tilted to the side, clearly not recognizing me at first. They hadn't seen me in almost three months. My face was partially hidden behind my mask (it was July 2021, and the COVID-19 pandemic was still ongoing), and I was much thinner, having lost over twenty pounds at that point. I was tan, and my hair was bleached from being out in the sun all day, every day. And the long hair and beard I had grown had me looking scraggly.

A moment later I saw the corners of their eyes crinkle into smiles, and my wife said in a high-pitched, excited tone, "What are you doing here?"

I wrapped my arms around all three of them in a big hug. My heart smiled as I embraced them. I had missed them so much.

Our five days in Tahoe seemed to pass in the blink of an eye. I was able to be present in the great moments we shared, but occasionally, the thought of having to leave them again and go back to the trail entered my mind. I knew it was going to hurt, and it did.

They brought me back to the trailhead I had come off near Donner Pass. The drive went by too fast. I tried to keep the conversations light and not let my emotions show too much. Turning into the parking lot where we would soon part ways broke my heart, and every smile and laugh after that point felt forced. It would be more than two months until we saw each other again.

We hiked a short stretch together on the PCT, about half a mile from the trailhead. Then I walked back with them, holding on to every second we had together. But it was time for me to go and for them to start their trip home; we couldn't wait any longer. We took a picture of us all standing together at a PCT trail marker sign, gave each other the last hugs and kisses, and then I watched them continue to the parking lot, get in the car, and drive away.

It was a terrible feeling, similar to saying goodbye and leaving for a deployment, and it hurt badly. I missed them more after they left than when they'd dropped me off at the airport to start my adventure.

Back on the trail, I did all I could to get my mind off missing my family. The afternoon heat and steep terrain leaving Donner Pass reminded me quickly of all I had enjoyed while in town: having a rental car, air conditioning, showers whenever I wanted, running water, a proper bed, and tons of restaurant options. But they were no more. It was time to embrace the suck again and put in some work.

A few miles later, I came up on a group of hikers sitting atop a ridge. I had heard airplanes flying around the area as I approached, and just as I walked up to the group and looked in the same direction they were, I saw two fire jumpers in the distance disappear into the trees near a small cloud of smoke. It was exciting to see parachutists since I took so much pride in my time as one in the air force.

Fire jumpers are a brave group of professionals combining two hazardous activities into one: jumping out of an airplane and fighting wildfires. But they have the additional challenge of wearing extremely heavy firefighting and protective equipment and having no fire trucks or quick way to escape if needed. I know it is far more technical than that, but that was how I viewed their world. I spent my years jumping trying not to land in the trees, while they spent their careers jumping into them on purpose.

The fire jumpers were out of our sight as soon as their parachutes went below the tree line, so I waited with the group of hikers, checking to see if the fire would grow, but it didn't. The smoke went away shortly after that, presumably because of the brave firefighters who jumped in to put it out, and I was soon on the trail again.

I went a few more miles before setting up camp, two ridges over from where the small fire was. I wasn't taking any chances and wanted some distance between me and the fire should it emerge again overnight, but it didn't.

Two more days passed. I approached the town of Sierra City, California. My experience on the trail started to change as I got further into Northern California. At first I was still on a high after leaving the spectacular views of the Sierra mountains and spending time with my family in Tahoe, despite how much I missed them after leaving. Now my grand views in the mountains were turning into views I didn't enjoy as much. The temperatures rose, reaching historic highs in some areas. The forest-fire season was also turning into a bad one, reaching record numbers and sizes in some areas. Some of the strong hikers I had met were beginning to question whether they should continue; a few had already left the trail. I even asked myself a few times, *Have I gotten everything I want out of this experience?* The answer was always no, and I never thought about quitting my hike, but I wasn't enjoying it as much as I had been. That was the start of what would turn out to be my most difficult stretch of trail, Northern California, and everything seemed to decline from there.

The next day, about ten miles out of Sierra City, the trail carried me along the top of a ridgeline for several miles. It was the highest ridgeline in the area, and I could see for miles. Coming around a bend in the trail, smoke from another fire came into my view, probably ten miles away from me to the east. It was enormous. I watched two firefighting aircraft drop their bright-red fire retardant on the flames. It appeared to have no impact at all. A steady flow of aircraft, including a specially equipped air force C-130, continued to battle the fire as I made my way along the ridge for the next few hours, but the fire continued to spread out of control.

I watched it grow quickly during my time on the ridge. I couldn't believe the size of the smoke cloud the fire produced. It was frightening. Even though there were several miles between me and the fire, I had never been that close to a forest fire, let alone one of that size. I was amazed at its power and how little the containment efforts were doing. I couldn't escape the view either; it was directly in my sight for hours, and I couldn't look away.

I would later learn that I was watching the beginnings of the Beckwourth Complex fires. The two fires, appearing to be one from my point of view, were started by lightning strikes days before and would eventually destroy over 105,000 acres—165 square miles—before being contained.

Witnessing the power of those fires got in my head. I had never seen something with such destructive power before. It terrified me. My mind was occupied with all things fire after that despite knowing what to do if I encountered one. I had researched and read up on the topic while preparing for the hike. But reading about it and seeing it are two different things.

*What will I do if I come over that next ridge and there's a fire in front of me? What happens if a fire starts or creeps up on me while I sleep? What if I get surrounded and trapped by a fire and can't escape? If I hit the SOS button on my inReach, will I get rescued before I'm burned alive?* Countless questions like those were constantly going through my mind. I'd never had thoughts of fear and worry consume me like that before; I'm just not wired that way.

After that, I stopped sleeping well. The slightest sounds at night would wake me. Snapping twigs, falling branches, and small animals moving near my tent—everything sounded like a fire. I didn't want to camp. I just wanted to keep moving. In my mind, moving and being able to see my surrounding area meant safety. Stopping, closing my eyes, or sleeping inside my tent meant danger.

Slowly, a few days after getting away from the Beckwourth fires, my mind started to calm down, and I became more aware of the trail and views around me again. But then I was hit with the next unpleasant surprise: another heat wave, the fifth that the other hikers and I had to endure. The temperatures were reaching the midnineties on the trail, but some towns at lower elevations were reaching the low hundreds. It was miserable to hike in those conditions, and there were points where I was concerned for my safety and that of the hikers I was around.

I needed a break from the heat and decided to stay overnight in the town of Quincy. I had to go there anyway to pick up a resupply box. Hundreds of firefighters from across the country were staged in Quincy to respond to the growing number of forest fires, making hotel rooms hard to come

Five Million Steps **111**

by, but I was lucky enough to get one of the last available rooms in town. I needed some time to cool off and research the weather and fire conditions for the next stretch of the trail.

It was 102 degrees when I got into town. I moved as quickly as I could to get my resupply box from the post office, grab some food to go from a nearby restaurant, and retreat to my room to sit in the air conditioning for the rest of the night.

The temperature dropped overnight, but it was ninety-one degrees the following morning when I left. I didn't want to hike anymore, but I continued. Coming out of Quincy, I reached my all-time low on the trail, spiraling down mentally and emotionally. I was no longer enjoying myself but instead putting in miles to escape my situation. I didn't want to talk to people, and I didn't want to share camps with anyone. I wanted everyone to leave me alone while I tried to get to a better place.

I thought I could shake it off, but my mental state got worse as I continued, and the darkness of my past returned to haunt me. The faces of fallen warriors flashed in my mind—thoughts of the pain their families experienced, echoes of shots and explosions that had injured or killed my brothers- and sisters-in-arms, and hearing over and over the last words I shared with men who later paid the ultimate sacrifice for our nation. I tried to push it down like I had years before, but I was alone and had nowhere to turn but the trail, which offered me no comfort or help. Like the Beckwourth fires, I had to simply watch the memories and hope I wouldn't be consumed. As I pushed forward, sun scorching me, sweat pouring down my face, and the air so hot it was hard to breathe, my thoughts kept returning to Afghanistan. Three incidents I experienced there had burned inside me for years.

The first occurred in 2002. I had deployed to Afghanistan to help establish security at one of the bases there and serve as a liaison between the air force and army units in the area. I was near my unit's control center,

**112**   Jason France

working a night shift, when we received news that two Americans had been shot when enemy forces ambushed them in another part of the country. They would be arriving soon by helicopter and needed to be transported to a building where a surgical team was preparing to treat their injuries, stabilize them, and prepare them to be transported to a US medical facility in Germany for more comprehensive care.

There were less than five hundred American and allied forces at the base, and I had one of the few trucks. I immediately drove to the flight line where the helicopter would land and met with another airman communicating with the inbound pilots. Two soldiers on ATVs pulled up to join us as we waited for the injured men to arrive.

It was one of the coldest months in Afghanistan, and in my rush to help, I ran out of the control center without grabbing my jacket. I stood there shivering as we waited for the helicopter to arrive, nervous about what was about to happen and hopeful that the two injured Americans would be okay. The war in Afghanistan was still new; US forces had only been there for a few months, and we were still experiencing many firsts and dealing with the unknowns that came with the beginning of a war.

It felt like we waited for hours before hearing the helicopter approaching in the distance. The base was in "blackout conditions" at night. No visible lights marked the runway, and forces on the base used night-vision devices or small red flashlights to prevent enemy forces from observing our activities and potentially targeting us. The airman guided the helicopter to our position, speaking to the pilots over his radio and using infrared chem light sticks to let them know where we were standing. The helicopter's side doors opened, and our small group ran up, grabbed the two litters holding the injured men, and carried them back to my truck.

Things happened quickly after that. We rushed them to the building where the surgical team was prepared to start their care. As we carried them inside the building, I saw the injured men for the first time in the

Five Million Steps **113**

light. Both had been bundled up in sleeping bags to keep them warm during transport, and both were motionless as we brought them into the makeshift operating room. I, and the others who helped transport them from the helicopter, left the room so the surgical team could get to work. I waited outside in the hallway, ready to move them again once the aircraft that was dispatched to transport them to Germany arrived.

More people started showing up as word about what happened traveled around the base. Some people needed to be there, key leaders and others directly involved to get them transported to Germany. But others, the curious onlookers, didn't need to be there and were only adding stress and confusion to the already stressful situation. I directed everyone who wasn't involved to go back outside.

Minutes later, two surgical team members brought one of the men out of the operating room. They placed him, still in the sleeping bag, on a table in the empty room next to where I was standing. He had died, and despite the surgical team's efforts, they were unable to revive him. Now they needed to focus all their efforts on the survivor.

Both medics dashed back toward the operating room, but I caught one of them just before reaching the door. "Hey, Doc, is there anything I can do to help?"

He paused for a split second, looking down, eyebrows furrowed. "Yeah, wait here a second," he replied before disappearing into the operating room. I caught a quick glance of the activity inside before the door slammed shut: four men surrounding the survivor, all working feverishly to treat his injuries, but also staying calm and focused.

The medic reemerged seconds later with a pack and some gear that belonged to the man who was killed. He quickly handed them to me and said, "Put this in the room with him, then stay on the door. And make sure no one goes in there" before rushing back into the operating room.

He was back inside before I finished saying, "I got it!"

**114** Jason France

I brought the items into the room and stood next to him for a moment. It was the first time I had seen someone who had been killed in combat. I had never met him before, but he was my brother. I felt like I had to say something—I owed it to him—but I couldn't find any words. It made me feel like shit. I overheard that he was married and had children. *What are they doing right now? How long will it take for them to learn about his death? What were the last words they said to each other?* I wasn't married yet; Monica and I had gotten engaged only weeks before I left for Afghanistan. I wasn't a father yet either, but my heart hurt for his family.

Back in the hallway, I got word that the other man had been stabilized, and the C-130 aircraft that would transport them would arrive soon. It was time to move them again. My truck was still parked just outside of the building. Two of us carried out the man who was killed. Two others carried out the man who had survived.

Things were different carrying those men the second time, though. Every detail became sharper, and I remember it all. The weight of the fallen warrior's body as we lifted him. The echo of my footsteps in the hallway as we brought him toward the main doors. How carefully we carried him out of the building, down the steps, and placed him in the truck bed. My rush of anger when I saw the group of onlookers gathered outside, one holding a camera high above his head to take photos. The jingle of my truck keys when I dropped them on the ground as I climbed into the driver's seat. Every bump on the road as we slowly drove to the flight line. The silhouettes of the aircrew in the back of the dimly lit aircraft as we approached. The clicking of the ratchet straps as we secured the litters to the plane's floor. The heat that warmed my face, and the smell of the exhaust as the C-130 taxied away.

And how quiet it was after the plane took off and I could no longer hear it. No wind, no sounds of vehicles, and no voices in the distance. It was dead silent.

Less than three weeks later, in that same truck, I helped unload and transport five Americans who had survived and two who had perished in a helicopter crash near the base. I had watched them taxi, take off, and head toward the mountains just before the crash.

A quick-reaction force responded to the crash site, recovered the injured and fallen Americans, and returned them to the base. Like the last incident, the survivors were treated and prepared to move to the same US medical facility in Germany. The fallen were prepared for their final journey home. Again, we brought them back to the flight line, loaded them all on a C-130, and watched as the plane departed.

I experienced similar emotions and feelings during that incident, but it was no easier than the first one. Seeing, carrying, and loading injured and deceased Americans in a combat zone doesn't get easier.

Almost two years later, I returned to Afghanistan for my second deployment there. I had already deployed once that year for the invasion of Iraq, and I was home only briefly before heading to Afghanistan. Deploying twice in the same year was difficult not only for me but for my wife as well. We had only been married for sixteen months, and I had been away more than home since our wedding. It was another tough deployment, and I was ready to get home to her.

It was my last day there. The plane taking me home had arrived; I'd checked in for my flight, checked my bags, and had three hours before departure. I went to the dining facility, only a short walk away, to have dinner before my long trip home. I wasn't sure when I would have the next chance for a hot meal. Ahead of me was a six-hour flight to Germany, where we would spend a few hours on the ground, and another flight of about eight and a half hours to the United States.

I got my food and was looking for a place to sit in the crowded seating area when I noticed a group of aviators sitting together at a long table. We didn't know each other, but we were part of the same task force, and I had seen them a few times before. They saw I was another task force member and invited me to sit with them. We made quick introductions and shared a brief but fun conversation, mostly about our experiences during the deployment but about our families too.

They finished their meals before me, and we said our quick goodbyes before they left. One said, "Safe travels home, brother. Enjoy that time with your wife" before walking away.

I returned to the passenger terminal after finishing my meal, flew out shortly after that, and had a smooth trip home. Two days after getting home, I saw on the news that an American helicopter had crashed in Afghanistan and the entire crew was killed. The report didn't include details about the crash, the type of helicopter, or the victims' names. Those details are not made public until the families of the fallen have been notified. There were hundreds of American helicopters in Afghanistan at the time, and although I was saddened by the news, I didn't think I had any connection with the victims.

Two days later, I saw another news report detailing the crash with the names and photos of the fallen. I recognized two of the men in the images, both part of the group I had shared dinner with just a few nights before, one being the man who wished me safe travels home. This incident was different for me than the other two, though. Their voices and laughter were still clear in my mind, and so were the smiles on their faces when they talked about their loved ones. These men I had seen alive.

Over the next four years, I deployed to Afghanistan twice more and Iraq twice more. With each deployment came tragedy and loss, some directly involving people I knew and others I didn't have a close connection with but still felt the pain of their loss. Even though we served in different services, specialties, and functions, we still shared the connection of serving our nation in combat.

Over time, though, I became almost numb to the emotions involved with death, people being injured, and the other bad things I experienced on my deployments. I protected myself through distraction and by keeping the emotions inside, thinking they would never revisit me.

Four more years and three assignments passed. I was promoted twice, reaching the highest enlisted rank in the air force. My wife was promoted as well. I didn't deploy during that time and knew it was unlikely I would ever deploy again. My wife deployed for the first time to Iraq. I was glad she didn't have to face as many horrible things as I had in that country, but she still faced a few and gained a better understanding of how experiences in a combat zone will change your life. She also gained a better understanding of how my experiences had affected me. And the best thing of all during that period was when we had our second son, making our beautiful family complete and bringing new joy into our lives. From the outside, our world looked perfect. But because of me, it was not.

The changes in my career took me away from the highs I had experienced for many years: jumping from airplanes, fast-roping from helicopters, firing all types of weapons, tough and realistic combat training and exercises, and of course, all the deployments—doing dangerous things in dangerous places, often facing the risk of serious injury or death. I didn't realize it when I was doing all those things, but I was addicted to the highs that came with them. I hadn't prepared to come down. I didn't even know I had to. The experience of deploying seven times in six years, knowing as soon as I got back from one I had to prepare for the next, kept me on the high. I never even had time to come down, let alone think about or prepare for what would happen when I did. And one day, it all caught up to me.

My family and I were having dinner together in our dining room. It was a typical dinner for us; nothing at all was out of the ordinary. We shared stories about our days; there were smiles and laughter. We were enjoying our time together as we always did. I was present, engaged, and in a great mood.

I still don't know what triggered my thoughts, but I found myself trying to remember the names of the people I knew who had died in combat. I was confused and didn't know why my mind was trying to recall those names. Within seconds I was sweating, my hands were shaking, and it was hard to breathe. I looked down at my plate, trying to control myself, hoping the thoughts would go away but still trying to remember the names at the same time. When I couldn't remember a single name, I completely broke down. I was crying uncontrollably and shaking even worse than before. I continued to look down at my plate and covered my face with my hands, embarrassed at how I was acting in front of my family. I wanted to get up and walk away but couldn't.

I didn't see her stand, but my wife moved beside me and put her hand on my shoulder. Her touch startled me. I jumped, lowered my hands, and looked up from my plate. I glanced over at my sons and saw looks of fear on their faces that I will never forget. That made my pain even worse. Standing behind me, my wife leaned down and put her arms around me, her face beside mine. The smell of her hair calmed me, and I slowly regained my composure. Once I could speak clearly, I did my best to explain to my family what had just happened and, most important to me at the time, apologized to my sons for scaring them. Discussing everything later with my wife, I told her I was feeling better and appreciated her being there for me.

It felt good to get out some of what I was feeling, and discussing it with my wife was helpful. But the fact that those thoughts came so quickly, with no warning, and I reacted the way I did, unable to control myself, scared me. All I could think about was *What will happen next time?*

Although I felt better that night, over the following days I had terrible headaches, was throwing up several times throughout the day, and barely had an appetite. I just wanted to sit somewhere quietly in the dark. But I still went to work, choosing not to take care of myself, and did my best to hide how I felt from my family, friends, and coworkers.

As time passed, I seriously considered what led to my breakdown. I quickly realized there had been signs for a long time, but I had either chosen to ignore them, my mind was tricking me into thinking I was fine, or I was making up reasons for why I shouldn't get help.

What did I do about it? Nothing. I continued to talk myself out of getting help whenever I was about to. I didn't want to be seen as a victim. I was more concerned about the stigma associated with mental health and how I thought others would view me than getting the care I needed. And I selfishly failed to consider how my issues affected my family.

I was raised in the "suck it up" culture of the security forces career field. To seek mental health care, or even say you needed it, was seen as a sign of weakness, whether anyone wanted to admit it or not. I was a newly promoted security forces chief master sergeant, and with that came an image I felt I had to uphold. *What would my young defenders or the other defender chiefs think about me if I go to the shrink?*

The stigma wasn't isolated to my career field, though. I had been a part of many discussions about dealing with the growing mental health crisis in the military and often saw the eye-rolling and look of "Are we talking about this again?" from others. They were the same people who would have quickly found out if I were seeking mental health care. *What will they think about me if I ask for help?* I felt entirely alone most times.

I was also worried about the future of my career. There were still emerging and changing policies associated with getting mental health care, and my mind quickly went to the worst-case scenarios. *Will I lose my security clearance? Will I not be able to handle firearms? Will I get removed from my career field? Will I be forced to retire?*

The thought of actually getting help scared me too. I didn't know what that help would look like. I saw it as a problem with no solution. It confused me when I thought about it, so I tried to avoid it.

I slowly reached a point, without even realizing it, where I couldn't feel happiness. My reactions were conditioned. I smiled and laughed at the right times, but I didn't actually feel happy. What I still felt, though, was the sadness associated with my experiences and having to hold it all in. I felt ashamed that I was hurting my family but doing nothing about it, felt guilty that I couldn't be happy during what should have been some of the happiest moments with my wife and sons. I felt the embarrassment of not being able to handle my problems and disappointment in myself for not having the strength to get help. I sometimes compared myself with others, thinking, *So many people have seen and experienced far worse things than I have, and they seem fine; my problems can't be that bad. What's wrong with me?*

I justified my failure to get help by making myself believe I couldn't be fixed. My lines of thought, using sadness as an example, typically went something like this:

*Sadness is all I can feel. If I fix the sadness, I will feel nothing. If I feel nothing, I can't feel happiness. If I can't feel happiness, I can't be a good husband and father. If I can't be a good husband and father, what good am I to my family? If I'm no good to my family, what good am I at all?*

*I'll continue to feel the sadness so I can at least feel something. My family will be fine. This will get better on its own over time.*

*I'm not going to get help.*

I also felt I was protecting my family by not sharing my struggles with them. I knew they would do anything to help me, but I didn't want to burden them with my problems. I didn't want them to hurt for me. I wanted to hold all my pain and sadness so they wouldn't have to. I didn't want them to know about some of the things I had seen and experienced. And I wanted to be strong for my sons, to protect their innocence, to let them be kids, and keep them sheltered from the bad things in the world. So I kept it all inside, believing I was doing what I had to do to protect myself and my family.

It was almost two years later when I finally reached out for help. I was the command chief master sergeant for the 75th Air Base Wing at Hill Air Force Base in Utah. I was holding the most senior enlisted leadership position for the second-largest base in the air force. It was my first assignment outside of my functional specialty. My assignments and opportunities throughout my career in security forces had prepared me for the responsibility and expectations of the new job; I was ready. The nomination, interview, and selection process went quickly, giving me little time to consider all that would change after stepping away from twenty-two years in security forces.

I quickly learned that although I was surrounded by great people in my new role, I was away from anyone who had similar experiences to mine. No one in my new circle understood me like my security forces brothers and sisters did, and I missed that. The way we supported each other, the things we joked about, and the ways we coped with the stresses of our job always made me feel a little better, sometimes just enough to get by. I was working hard and doing my best for the people I served in my new position, but I still felt out of place and alone most of the time.

Soon the terrible headaches I had experienced before returned. Then my sleep suffered; I woke up several times every night feeling worried and uneasy but didn't know what about. I was constantly tired, close to the point of exhaustion. I lost my ability to focus; my thoughts were always scattered. I became overwhelmed sometimes and found it difficult to complete the simplest tasks. My memory suffered too, and I had to write most everything down so I wouldn't forget details and small things. It became difficult to stay calm and patient with people and control my temper. I knew it was only a matter of time before I blew up and possibly did or said something I would regret or permanently change things at work or home. And still, recognizing all those things and knowing I needed to get help, I didn't. I went on for months more, trying to figure out how to fix myself as my confidence faded and my helplessness grew.

One night I finally reached the point where I realized I couldn't get better on my own. My wife and I were having dinner at a restaurant when another issue I was facing, my hypervigilance, consumed me worse than it ever had before. We were seated where I could face the restaurant's entrance like always. As we ate and talked, I completely checked out. I heard everything around me, but I couldn't hear her. I was looking all around, feeling I had to look at every face in the room and see everyone who entered the restaurant. I forgot that where I should be looking was at my wife, sitting right in front of me. When I finally looked at her, her expression told me she knew I hadn't heard anything she'd said, and it was true. I hadn't.

But it wasn't that I didn't want to hear her; I just couldn't. I saw her lips moving, but I couldn't hear her words. I heard the hostess greeting the guests twenty-five feet away. I heard every word of the conversation between the couple two tables behind me. I heard the sounds in the kitchen, utensils touching plates, and everything else—all except my wife's words as she sat before me.

She looked me in the eyes for a moment, shook her head, looked down, and continued to eat. It hurt to see how I had made her feel, and all I could think was *You're an asshole. She deserves better than this. Handle your shit. Fix yourself.*

I was physically and mentally exhausted when we left the restaurant, typical of how I felt after being around large groups of people I didn't know. She said nothing to me on our drive home. I deserved that. Walking in the door when we got home, I watched her greet and hug our sons. All three of them, still sharing their embrace, looked over at me. I was still standing near the door, close but also far away. They looked at me as if I were a stranger. The picture of them together, and the way they looked at me, broke my heart. I didn't feel I deserved to be a part of their embrace. That was the lowest moment for me in my struggles with mental health.

Five Million Steps    123

CHAPTER 12

# THE PATH TO HEALING

The following morning, I attended our wing's staff meeting. It was held once a week and attended by the commanders and key leaders from the organizations across our wing, about twenty-five people altogether. Colonel Clark, the medical group (hospital) commander, was one of those commanders. I had formed a great relationship with him over the time we had worked together. I admired him a lot. He was a respected leader, trustworthy, humble, and approachable, a genuinely kind person who took great care of his people. I planned to talk to him after the meeting to let him know I would be contacting the mental health clinic and get any advice he had to offer on my situation.

I got nervous the moment I saw Colonel Clark as we gathered in the room and took our seats. *You know you need to do this. You know they'll take care of you. All you have to do is ask.*

The meeting started, and we followed the standard sequence of program updates, metrics briefs, highlights of activities from the past week, projected activities and events, and discussions on important issues in the wing. During the entire meeting, my thoughts were consumed by my fear of asking for help and being perceived as weak. *Everyone on the base is going to find out about this. What are they going to think? What do I even say? "Hey, Doc, I'm all fucked up. Can you fix me?"* I even caught my mind telling me again that I didn't need help.

*Dude, you got this. Just suck it up. You'll be fine.*

I don't remember a single word that was spoken during the meeting. The whole hour passed by in what seemed to be seconds. As the command chief, I always had the opportunity to provide my remarks at the end of the meeting, just before the commander's closing comments. When that time came, I was so wrapped up in the argument I was having with myself in my head that I didn't realize it was my turn to speak. I was just staring down at the blank page in my notebook. I was brought back to the room when my commander reached over and put her hand on my forearm. "Chief, are you with us? What do you have?"

Her touch startled me. I jumped and almost said out loud what I was thinking: *No, you're not going to be fine!* But thankfully, the words didn't come out. The room was silent when I came to my senses. Looking down the long table, I realized all eyes were on me, waiting for me to say something. All I could come up with was, "No, ma'am. Nothing for the group this morning" before looking back down at my notebook.

The commander concluded the meeting with her remarks. Following the military tradition of paying respect to her position as the commander, we all rose from our seats and stood at attention for a brief moment before people broke away for the typical sidebar conversations or to leave the room. Still standing near my seat, I made eye contact with Colonel Clark. He was standing directly across from me. My heart was racing, I was nauseous, my hands were sweaty, and my feet felt so heavy that it was hard to pick them up to move. And once I could, I thought about just walking away. *You don't need anyone's help.* But the picture of my family from the night before flashed in my mind again. I couldn't avoid it any longer. It was time.

Making my way around the table to Colonel Clark, I quietly asked,

"Hey, sir. You got a minute?"

"Of course. What's up, chief?" he replied with a look of concern, stepping away from the small group of people who remained near the table.

"I'm having a hard time, and I need help. I wanted to let you know that I'll be calling mental health this morning, and I don't want you to be surprised when you find out."

That was the first time I had said the words "I need help" out loud, and I was hit with an immediate sense of relief. The tension in my neck and shoulders, the knots in my stomach, and the tightness in my chest that had been present for as long as I could remember eased just a bit, enough to let me know I had made the right decision. I was proud to have taken the first step in getting the help I needed.

I shared a few more details about what I was experiencing and answered the questions he needed to ask to make sure I wasn't in crisis. He even offered to bring me to the clinic himself. I declined and assured him that although eager to meet with the mental health team, I could wait for a scheduled appointment. Our conversation finished with him assuring me his team would take care of me. I already knew they would, but seeing the look of sincerity on his face and hearing him say it gave me an additional sense of relief.

By the time I got back to my office on the other side of the base, less than thirty minutes later, a message was already waiting for me from the mental health clinic. I called back immediately and was scheduled for an appointment later that day. They told me I could enter through the side door of the building instead of the main entrance, where other patients might see me, and I could wear civilian clothes to reduce the chance of anyone recognizing me. Almost everyone on the base knew who I was; my photo was even on the wall at the clinic entrance, next to photos of the base's other senior leaders. They wanted to prevent any embarrassment they thought I might have by coming to their clinic. I appreciated their thoughtfulness,

Five Million Steps  **127**

but after finally getting past my initial nervousness of admitting I needed help, I wasn't concerned about embarrassment. It was time to get moving on my path to healing. I was also happy to get an appointment so soon so I wouldn't try to convince myself again that I didn't need help.

My first appointment consisted of completing a series of intake forms to explain the issues I was experiencing and meeting with a psychologist to discuss them. It was my first time ever speaking to a psychologist as a patient. It felt good to share my struggles with him, and he gave me hope, even during the first appointment, that I could get better.

At my next appointment the following day, I completed an assessment to determine if I was suffering from post-traumatic stress disorder (PTSD). Despite overcoming my fear of seeking mental health care, the thought of being diagnosed with PTSD worried me. I was still concerned with the stigma as well as any potentially negative impacts on my career. I struggled to answer all the assessment questions honestly, wanting to enter what I thought were the "right" answers in some areas instead of the honest answers. Ultimately, I was diagnosed with generalized anxiety disorder (GAD), not PTSD.

After I received my diagnosis, the psychologist and I discussed my assessment results. He explained several treatment options that had been successful for others with GAD. A treatment he had seen with some of the best results for cases like mine was prolonged exposure (PE) therapy, a specific type of cognitive behavioral therapy. He explained that for many people, PE reduced recurring thoughts, flashbacks, and avoidance behaviors associated with traumatic events, all of which I was experiencing frequently. He also explained that it could help improve my quality of life, specifically with my relationships with family, friends, and coworkers. And finally, he explained how it could provide me with some skills to help manage the triggers, behaviors, and emotions that were impacting me in so many ways.

I was all in. PE therapy sounded like exactly what I needed, and I wanted to start as soon as possible. I was referred to a psychologist off base, someone in the local community who specialized in that type of therapy.

My first appointment with her was the following week. She had recently separated from the air force and started her own practice. I'd met her a year earlier, while she was still in uniform, and seen her in action before she separated. She was part of a groundbreaking mental health support program our base was testing for the air force. Her impact on people with issues like mine was remarkable, and I was lucky to be one of her patients. We connected well immediately.

During that first appointment, she explained in great detail the different ways anxiety can manifest and how it can impact people in different ways. It was as if she was reading from a checklist of symptoms I was experiencing. Recurring memories of and thoughts about traumatic experiences, feelings of guilt that I could have done more to help, always feeling like something bad was about to happen, hypervigilance, difficulty concentrating and remembering things, getting angry at seemingly insignificant things, headaches, poor sleep—the list went on. She described what I was experiencing perfectly before we even started the first therapy session. She also explained the reality of the highs and lows that patients sometimes face during PE therapy, that my thoughts and feelings may get worse before getting better. I was nervous but ready.

Near the end of our first appointment, she asked me what I thought was causing my anxiety and the manifestations that would typically follow. Memories of the three events I described in the previous chapter were the common factor in my most anxious periods, so those events were the main focus of our sessions over the following months.

We started each session with me identifying a memory that was particularly troubling and causing symptoms I wanted to gain control over. Then, with my eyes closed, I explained each traumatic event from the first-person point of view. She guided me through it, asking questions and encouraging

Five Million Steps **129**

me to share every detail, emotion, thought, and sensation.

To have the memories in my head was one thing. To recall and explain them out loud in painful detail was another. We went into such detail in our sessions that I sometimes felt as if I were reliving the events. I would sweat, tremble, feel nauseous, and break down in tears in some of our sessions. But after each one, I felt a little bit better, and my hope for healing increased.

Sometimes the sessions focused on situations in my daily life that were causing me anxiety. Those discussions were a little easier for me, and I quickly learned that there were similarities in how my mind processed stressful situations I'd faced in combat and stressful situations I faced in daily life, driving similar reactions. Drawing the two together made the path to recovery seem less overwhelming.

The toughest part of the therapy for me, though, was the homework. I was required to record our sessions with my phone and play the recordings to myself repeatedly between each session. As if explaining each event in the first person wasn't difficult enough, repeatedly listening to myself on the recordings presented a level of difficulty I never knew existed. Although they were audio recordings, I liken the experience to watching a scene in a movie that becomes so uncomfortable that you want to fast-forward to the next scene or turn it off completely. It was so hard to listen to myself on those recordings at first. But over time, listening became easier, reliving the experiences in the recordings became less painful, and my anxiety level started to decrease.

As my sessions progressed, I noticed other ways the therapy was helping me. My worry and guilt were subsiding; my focus, sleep, mental clarity, and memory were improving; I was connecting better with my family, coworkers, and friends; and I began to feel happiness again. I knew I would never be "cured," but my experience with prolonged exposure therapy gave me tools I could use for the rest of my life to help keep my anxiety under control. The thought that I might struggle again someday with the same

**130** Jason France

issues was always there, but I wouldn't have imagined they would resurface eight years later on the Pacific Crest Trail.

• • •

The trail continued to punish me as I trudged north from Quincy. The relentless heat and smoke-filled air were killing my endurance, and the miles became far more difficult the further I moved north, making it seem impossible to recover from the work I was putting in. The overgrown and poorly maintained sections of trail, sometimes miles long, were frustrating the hell out of me, slowing my movement and reducing the number of miles I could hike each day. The news of fires spreading closer to the trail and the threat of new fires emerging in my path got in my head again, spiking my anxiety and making it impossible for me to sleep. My mental clarity and sharpness were also declining as my exhaustion grew. As hard as I tried, I couldn't find anything positive around me. I just kept getting pushed deeper into the hole I was in, struggling to enjoy anything about the experience.

I saw how everything was impacting the other hikers too. The conversations we had that were once fun and full of laughter had turned into sharing news about fires, heat waves, and trail closures; information from forest and national park service rangers; plans to skip forward to get away from the fires and smoke; and talk of other hikers who had decided to leave the trail altogether. I continued pushing, though, convinced that conditions could only improve.

Two days later, with fifty of the toughest miles behind me and only about ten miles until the town of Chester for an overnight stop and resupply, I was briefly lifted out of my hole when I reached the PCT's halfway point. I was elated when I rounded a corner and saw the midway-point marker. The simple gray post is about three feet tall, four by four inches, and says "PCT midpoint" on the side facing the trail. "CANADA 1,325 miles" is on the north side, and "MEXICO 1,325 miles" is on the south.

The trail provided exactly what I needed at that moment. I celebrated alone at the marker, sitting in silence, exhausted but smiling, and squeezed a melted Snickers bar from its wrapper into my mouth. Then I finished my push to the trailhead at California Highway 36, where I caught a quick hitch into Chester. I continued my celebration in town with tacos, beer, and ice cream before shopping for my resupply, cleaning up, and relaxing for a night in my hotel. The following morning, I caught another quick hitch back to the trailhead, where I was met with a smooth trail and a much-needed break in the heat—only fifty-five degrees. Things were looking up.

Three days later, though, I was hit again with more smoke and heat. I also received news that the day after I left Chester, a new forest fire started, the Dixie Fire. It ended up being the largest fire in California that year, and the second largest in the state's history. It destroyed over 960,000 acres and burned over 600 homes. A hundred-mile section of the PCT was closed the day after I passed through it, including access to the midway point. I was one of the last hikers to touch the midway point marker before that section closed. While I felt terrible for the hikers who were unable to celebrate reaching the midpoint, I also felt fortunate to have been able to do so myself.

I continued up the trail, and the trail continued to suck. I faced more extreme heat and more smoke, breathing it in and having my views obstructed. My anxiety remained, driven by my newly found fear of fire. I still wasn't enjoying my hike, and my focus stayed on putting miles behind me so I could get out of California.

As I pushed through the final miles of Northern California, I finally started to realize the positive side of the experience. The trail was forcing me to stay in my thoughts. I had no option but to face the darkness and trauma of my past. I had no grand mountain views or beautiful scenery to provide distraction or escape. I had nowhere to go but north and deeper into my thoughts. Similar to my experience in PE therapy—where I had to listen to my sessions over and over—my daily struggles on the trail became easier to endure, the thoughts from my past less painful, and the anxiety created by it all less intense.

Finally leaving California and crossing into Oregon was a surreal experience for me. It seemed like I had been in California forever. I'd experienced so much growth as a hiker and as a person during the three months I'd spent there. While I was relieved to be in a new state and a new section of trail, I knew I wouldn't have been able to appreciate it as much if it weren't for the challenges I overcame in those first seventeen hundred miles.

Stepping across the border, I was greeted with light rain, a breeze, and a drop in temperature. The harshness of Northern California was now behind me, and Oregon welcomed me with a fresh start. About two miles in, I found trail magic: a cooler of beer and sodas and a chair under a tree. The tree protected me from the rain while I waited out the shower and drank a beer. Coincidentally, the chair faced back toward California.

The view of it from my seat brought me a sense of calm. I realized that despite all its challenges, Northern California had given me a gift: the gift of time. Time to process. Time to think. Time to accept that in every traumatic event I experienced during my many deployments, I had no control over what happened. I did everything I could, and nothing would have changed the outcomes.

Northern California allowed me to see that, despite extensive therapy, I was still viewing those events through the eyes of the young man I used to be. Now it was time to shift my perspective to that of the man I was today—more mature and experienced with a deeper understanding of the complex world we live in, the sacrifices that can come with serving our nation, the value of life, and the different ways we deal with the pain of loss.

Northern California gave me hell, but it also gave me the time I had never given myself to heal.

CHAPTER 13

# OVERCOMING THE OBSTACLES

Crater Lake National Park was one of the areas I looked forward to the most during my hike. I had never been there but found the photos and videos of the lake and its surroundings to be absolutely incredible. After hiking twenty-eight miles, I entered the park's southern boundary late in the day. I was tired but kept pushing hard so I could make it to Mazama Village. I had a resupply package waiting for me at the Annie Creek Restaurant and Gift Shop, and I had to hurry if I wanted to get there before the gift shop closed. I was also excited to get dinner at the restaurant, as I hadn't carried much food since my last resupply two days ago. I was starving.

I made it to the gift shop minutes before they closed and picked up the resupply box that would carry me eighty-five miles to my next stop, Shelter Cove Resort. Fortunately, the restaurant stayed open later than the gift shop, and I was able to enjoy a big dinner without being rushed. Two cheeseburgers, a pulled-pork sandwich, and a bowl of elk chili nearly filled me up. I got a pepperoni pizza to go before making my way to the nearby campground, where PCT hikers were allowed to camp for free. At least thirty other hikers were there when I arrived, but I was exhausted and kept to myself as I set up my tent, threw my pack inside, and put my unopened resupply box in one of the camp's bear lockers. I struggled to stay awake as I ate half of my pizza and gave the rest to another hiker. I was in my tent and off to sleep after that. Despite the crowd of hikers in camp, I didn't wake up once during the night.

I awoke the next morning refreshed and excited to see Crater Lake. The lake is north of Mazama Village, and since I entered the park from its southern boundary, I hadn't been near it yet. I was in no hurry to get back on the trail and up to the lake too early, though. I wanted to break camp, pack up all my resupply items, and eat breakfast at the restaurant without having to rush. I also didn't want to get to the lake too early. My plan was to start hiking about an hour before sunset that night. The Perseid meteor shower was nearing its peak, and I was going to hike away from the crowds, stealth camp near the rim of the lake near a place called Devil's Backbone, watch the sunset, see the meteor shower, and watch the sunrise the following morning, all from the same spot. Even though camping on the rim of Crater Lake was not allowed, I saw it as a once-in-a-lifetime opportunity and was willing to risk getting caught by the park rangers to make it happen.

I finally made it up to Rim Village that afternoon after some creative hiking. I got a ride up to the rim, slack packed (hiking without a pack) back down to Mazama Village where my pack was waiting, and got another ride back up to the rim with my pack, all to get the miles in without skipping any of the trail.

I was awestruck the moment I saw the lake. The conditions were perfect. The smoke that had been lingering in the area had dissipated. When I arrived, there was a clear blue sky, visibility for miles around, beautiful trees and rocks, and a clear view of the deep blue lake. It was everything I had imagined, and it was even better to stand on the rim and see it all in front of me. The photos and videos I had seen before did it no justice. I had cell

**136** Jason France

reception near Rim Village, too, and shared the beautiful views with my family on FaceTime. It was one of the highlights of my hike.

I spent the afternoon exploring the area, talking to other hikers and tourists, eating lunch at the café at Rim Village, and relaxing as I waited patiently for the right time to start my hike to Devil's Backbone for the awesome night I had planned.

Talking with one of the park rangers near Rim Village, I learned that the smoke and air quality were projected to worsen in the coming days. That worried me. The effects of hiking through so much smoke in the previous weeks were hitting me hard. I had persistent sinus pain and chest congestion, my eyes were swollen, I kept getting nosebleeds, I was constantly coughing, and I had terrible headaches nearly every day. My stubbornness prevented me from doing anything about it, but I knew I couldn't endure it much longer without a break. *I just need to make it to Shelter Cove, and I'll be good. It's clear up there.*

Just after 4:30 p.m., though, as I started my hike on the rim trail, the wind shifted, and smoke started coming over the north rim of the lake, cascading down toward the water and filling the sky with the familiar gray haze I had been enduring for weeks.

*You have got to be shitting me.*

It was the first step in the chain of events that turned one of my best days on the trail into one of the worst. Within an hour, I couldn't see the lake clearly from the rim. I knew my plans for the night were ruined. I also knew I couldn't subject my body to those conditions any longer. It was time for me to get out of there and move up the trail and away from the smoke.

I messaged a local trail angel with my inReach. She responded quickly, understanding the conditions we hikers were facing and happy to help. We arranged to meet the next morning where the trail intersected with a highway less than ten miles ahead. I was torn. On one hand, I knew I was doing the right thing by taking care of myself and moving out of the smoke. On the other hand, I was disappointed that I would miss seventy miles of trail. I had hiked over eighteen hundred miles without missing any open sections of trail and was hoping to hike every available mile on the entire PCT.

The next available campground, Grouse Hill, was four easy miles away, less than two hours over smooth terrain. I'd packed a beer to drink at Devil's Backbone later that night while watching the meteor shower. Since my plan was ruined, I popped it open and drank it as I made my way toward camp, instead watching the eerie red sunset through the haze. Even though my plans changed, it didn't mean I had to put my beer to waste.

I made it to camp after dark and quietly set up my tent using my headlamp. The beam showed that the smoke was thicker here than near the lake. There were other tents scattered around the area, but everything was quiet. I fell asleep still thinking about how disappointing it was to miss those seventy miles.

I woke up at 2:30 a.m., coughing and having difficulty breathing. It was completely dark, and I wasn't sure where I was for a few seconds. The first thing I noticed once I realized I was in my tent was a heavy smell of smoke, even heavier than when I got into camp. I sat up and held perfectly still, resisting the strong urge to cough as I listened for any crackles or pops that could mean a fire nearby. Nothing. I looked around the walls of my tent for any glow shining through. Again, nothing. I was holding my breath and heard my heart beating fast in my ears. I let out a hard cough and immediately felt a splitting pain in my head. I was in bad shape.

I put on my headlamp, unzipped the mesh door to my tent, opened one side of the vestibule, and rolled onto my hands and knees to look outside. Not turning on my headlamp yet, I looked around to check again for any glow of a fire. A sense of relief came over me when I saw none.

When I turned on my headlamp, the beam showed smoke in every direction—again, thicker than I'd seen when I got into camp. I still didn't think a fire was close, but I wasn't taking any chances. I dressed and left my tent, wanting a better look around the area to make sure.

I moved as quietly as I could and kept my headlamp pointed toward the ground as I passed the other tents and got onto the main trail. I jogged a quarter mile in each direction and was relieved to find nothing but smoke. My eyes were stinging, my throat was burning, and I was still struggling to breathe. I slowed down to catch my breath as I approached the small trail leading back to camp. I wiped what I thought was condensation off my mustache, then noticed a metallic smell when I inhaled. I looked at my hand. It wasn't wet from condensation; it was blood.

Back in my tent and unable to sleep, I thought about my situation and made peace with my decision to get help and move forward. I also realized that I was so wrapped up in my pride and stubbornness that I had completely disregarded my health and safety. I was more worried about getting in all the miles.

The next morning, the trail angel met me and seven other hikers at the road intersection. She brought us north to Shelter Cove, out of the smoke. It was clear there, and within a matter of days, I started to feel healthy again. No more headaches, congestion, or coughing; my sleep and mental clarity improved; and my body recovered quickly again from the physical exertion. I didn't fully realize what bad shape I was in before moving north. I had just overcome another obstacle the PCT threw at me: the decision to swallow my pride and miss seventy miles of the trail. However, I was better for it and enjoyed the experience even more because of my decision.

Like many people, the obstacles I've had to overcome throughout my life have made me stronger and helped shape me into the person I am today. One of the biggest obstacles I faced while growing up—difficulty in school—became a blessing in disguise later in life.

The importance of education was never instilled in me growing up. It was a topic that was never even discussed at home. Essentially, starting in

Five Million Steps **139**

elementary school, I was conditioned to not care about my performance in school. When I came home, I would turn off all thoughts about school and do whatever I wanted, never considering or understanding the negative effects I would experience in the future by not focusing on my education. I don't remember ever being asked about the classes I was taking, if I had homework, or if I needed help. There were no discussions about my grades when my report cards arrived. I was never questioned about or held accountable for my poor grades. I was never encouraged to do better. I received nothing to inspire or encourage me to put effort into school.

The first time I remember being worried about my grades was in fifth grade. My teacher told us that report cards had been sent home, and I knew mine would be at my house in a few days. I also knew I hadn't done well and that report card would show it. I was nervous, but more about getting in trouble than the grades I received. Thinking about it kept me awake. I ran home from school every day after that to check the mailbox for my report card. I was relieved on the days that it wasn't there but also anxious for the anticipation to be over. Finally, it arrived. My heart jumped when I saw the envelope containing my report card. I thought about throwing it away but got scared and put it back in the mailbox at the bottom of the stack.

I was sitting on the couch in our living room, watching television, when my mom walked past me on her way to our mailbox on the front porch. I was trying not to act suspicious, keeping my eyes on the television and not making eye contact with her. She got the mail, came back inside, and opened the first piece as she walked past me again and into the kitchen.

I saw her through the doorway, standing near our kitchen table with her back to me. I heard her rip open the next two envelopes, take out the contents, and set each piece on the table. My report card was next. *Here it comes.* But like the other envelopes, she opened it, looked at my report card, set it on the table, and went about her business like nothing had happened.

I wasn't sure what to expect, but it certainly wasn't that: nothing. *Okay, she's going to let me have it later tonight.* But the evening came and went with no mention of my report card. Through the eyes of my fifth-grade self, I was excited and relieved. *I'm not in trouble!* Not only was I relieved, but it also showed me that she didn't care what kind of grades I received. That didn't bother me at all at the time. Years later, though, through the eyes of my adult self and the eyes of a parent, everything about that event is extremely disappointing.

It wasn't until my senior year in high school that I worried about my grades again. Near the end of my first semester, I learned I was one credit shy of what I needed to graduate, even if I passed all my classes that semester and the next. I had failed too many classes. My focus throughout high school was on work. Sometimes I held two jobs at once, and they pulled me even further away from caring about my grades. Work provided me with the money I needed to get by. School didn't.

The only option I had to earn the one credit I needed was to be a teacher's aide for driver's education during my last semester. My high school's driver's education classes were held before the regular school day started. I came in at 6:50 a.m. every morning, graded tests, recorded scores, and did other administrative tasks the teacher needed. It was easy, and I didn't learn anything by doing it, but it allowed me to graduate.

I graduated from high school with a 1.7 grade point average. I didn't get a single A during my four years of high school, but I did earn six Fs. As embarrassing as it is to admit, I just didn't understand the importance of doing well in school until it was almost too late. I have no one to blame but myself, but I was written off by everyone around me, including my teachers. The best example of how some of my teachers must have viewed me was a comment one of them wrote in my yearbook at the end of my senior year: "Jason, it's nice to know that you liked my class so much that you wanted to fail so you could have me two years in a row. Thanks for the compliment!" He laughed when he handed my yearbook back to me after signing it. I laughed too, thinking it was funny then, but it's not. Not once did he ask if I needed help. Not once did he ask why I was doing so poorly. Not once did he show any concern for me at all.

His comment stuck with me. I didn't take it to heart at the time, but later in life, as a supervisor, a leader, an educator, and a father, I used his actions and words as an example of how not to treat people. He taught me more about life in the thirty-one words he wrote in my yearbook than I could have ever learned from him during two semesters of his literature class.

The obstacles I faced in school pushed me to become more disciplined in my future academic pursuits, and the rewards soon followed. I earned distinguished graduate awards at every level of professional military education, graduated with honors from college, instructed at four academic institutions throughout my military career, and have worked as an adjunct professor for the air force since retiring. The most important part, though, is I can recognize the struggles of others, connect with them, help them navigate and overcome their struggles, and see them succeed.

A second example of a challenge I overcame was a personal and professional endeavor I spent over six years pursuing: graduating United States Army Ranger School and earning my ranger tab. Ranger school is the army's premier small-unit tactics and leadership school. It is one of the most demanding schools in the military and, by design, pushes students to their limits, physically and mentally, under extreme conditions of fatigue, hunger, and sleep deprivation. When I went through it, it was sixty-two days long, it was conducted in three phases at different locations, and it had an attrition rate of about 75 percent.

The first ranger graduates I met were at the army's Jungle Warfare School at Fort Sherman, Panama, in 1993. I was stationed at Howard Air Force Base, also in Panama, and our squadron received a few slots for each jungle warfare class. I was selected to lead our four-person team for the three-week course. We were attached to an infantry company sent there

**142** Jason France

from the 101st Airborne Division at Fort Campbell, Kentucky.

After some lighthearted jokes and service rivalry jabs, my team and I were accepted into their tribe. The two leaders of the platoon we were assigned to a lieutenant and a sergeant first class; both wore ranger tabs on the left shoulders of their uniforms. I noticed immediately that there was something different about them. Their confidence, knowledge, appearance, and leadership presence were incredible, like nothing I had ever seen in the leaders I'd been exposed to in my three years in the air force. The respect their soldiers had for them was remarkable too.

I was a young, emerging leader, and although I was cocky, I was eager to learn, so I watched their every move, listened intently to every word they said, and learned as much as I could from them in the short time we were together.

When I returned to my unit after graduating, I spoke to the sergeant who oversaw our squadron's training office about my experiences in the course and my interactions with the ranger-qualified leaders. He told me that the air force is allowed to attend ranger school and that there is a three-week selection course, pre-ranger, held at Indian Springs Air Force Auxiliary Field, Nevada (now Creech Air Force Base), twice a year.

"How do I get into the next class?" were the next words out of my mouth.

A few months later, and after an enormous amount of preparation, I was standing in the middle of the Nevada desert, wondering what I had gotten myself into. Students had come from all over the world to attend this course. The instructors, all ranger qualified, had come from across the air force too, and their job was to make sure that the air force sent only the best candidates to ranger school. The air force only gets six slots per year, and the airmen will not only go to school to earn their ranger tabs, but they will also represent our entire service at one of the toughest schools in the military.

The intensity and pace of pre-ranger was something I had never experienced. The physical and mental stress, high expectations and standards of performance, and intentional chaos and confusion were all part of the experience to ensure we were prepared for what we would face at ranger school.

I injured myself on the second day of the course during the daytime land navigation evaluation in the desert. The land navigation evaluations, one day and one night, are done alone to ensure each student can navigate on their own. I was doing well, had found the fourth of six points I needed to find, and was moving to my fifth point. As I was climbing out of a ravine I had just crossed, the ground gave way, and I fell about six feet back to the bottom. I landed on my right foot, with my leg fully extended and knee locked. The impact of my fall, and the position of my leg, caused my knee to bend about forty-five degrees out to the side. I heard a pop and felt a grinding sensation in my knee as I crumpled over and came to a rest on top of my injured leg. Rolling onto my back, my knee popped back into place. I didn't feel the pain for a few seconds, but I knew I had injured myself badly and that my time at pre-ranger was done.

It took me nearly three hours to hobble and crawl the two miles back to the training compound where we started. I was eventually brought to a nearby hospital, where I learned that I had torn my anterior cruciate ligament. I flew back home to Panama two days later.

After a year of recovery and physical therapy, I was stronger and faster than before and was back at pre-ranger for the second time. It was the beginning of the third week. I had passed all my individual evaluations and was being evaluated as the platoon leader during a simulated combat patrol. The platoon leader position is one of the four graded leadership positions that students rotate through, typically for a twelve-hour period, before different students take the positions and are evaluated. Every student must pass at least two leadership evaluations to be considered for one of the slots at ranger school.

At that point in the course, we were all worn out from only getting about two hours of sleep and eating once a day. We were drained from the other physical and mental demands of the course and the effects of being in the desert conditions, hot in the day and cold at night. The stresses of the course affect people in different ways. The lack of food is what got to most of the people in my class. The lack of sleep is what got to me. I was hallucinating sometimes and fell asleep if I stopped moving for too long. A few times I even fell asleep while walking. When I snapped out of it, I had no idea where I was or how I got there.

Falling asleep will get anyone in trouble, but falling asleep during an evaluation is an automatic failure. I fell asleep on that patrol, and I failed. The instructor who caught me was both angry and disappointed. I was doing well up to that point and was on the path of getting one of the six slots to go to ranger school. I let my team down, I let my instructors down, and I let myself down. I finished the course the following week, technically graduating, but it was no surprise when I was told I didn't get selected for one of the ranger school slots. "See you next year" is what I got, and I deserved it.

Another year passed, and I went back a third time. I had learned a lot from my two previous experiences and was in the best shape I had ever been. My academics were solid, and I felt that nothing would stop me. Nothing except the groin injury I got from throwing dozens of heavy bags and packs into the back of a truck on the first night. On the morning of the second day, I was unable to complete the five-mile run under the forty-minute time requirement, taking fifty minutes when I normally ran it in just over thirty. I was medically dropped from the course and told "See you next year" once again. I was frustrated, but not defeated, and got back to recovering and training as soon as I got home.

Finally, another year later, after my fourth time attending pre-ranger school, I was selected for one of the six slots to ranger school after passing all my graded evaluations and helping my classmates make it through.

Exactly six years from the day I started my first pre-ranger course, I was standing at Camp Rogers in Fort Benning, Georgia, (now Fort Moore) for the first day of ranger school. I was the only air force student in a class of over 350 students, and all eyes were on me. One of the first comments I received from a ranger instructor (RI), Staff Sergeant Ferris, was, "What are you even doing here, Air Force? This is not for you." I knew I would have to watch my every move and prove myself even more than the other students. It didn't bother me, though. I had prepared for six years, and nothing would break my confidence. I planned to pass every evaluation the first time and go straight through the course without being "recycled," the term used when a student fails a phase and has to start over with the next class.

The first evaluation was the Ranger Physical Assessment, a test where every student had to do forty-nine push-ups in two minutes, do fifty-nine sit-ups in two minutes, finish a two-mile run in under fourteen minutes and fifty-two seconds, and do six chin-ups. I knew I could do over a hundred push-ups and sit-ups without stopping, run two miles in under twelve minutes, and do over twenty strict chin-ups in a minute. I didn't think I would have any problems with the physical assessment. As luck would have it, though, Sergeant Ferris, the same RI who asked me why I was there, saw me as our class prepared for the assessment.

"Hey, Air Force, make sure you get in my line for push-ups," he said with a big grin.

"Roger that, sergeant," I replied sarcastically, also with a big grin.

Nostrils flared and eyebrows scrunched together, he fired back, "You're going to the house today, Air Force. I can feel it."

"Not today, sergeant!" I shouted even more sarcastically and with a bigger smile.

"We'll fucking see about that."

And with that, the games began. Getting over 350 students through the physical assessment was no small feat. There had to be over fifty RIs counting, timing, recording results, and orchestrating the chaos to get everyone through. There were probably fifteen stations evenly spaced along the center of a mulch-covered area, each with an RI and a line of students. The first evaluation was for push-ups. The first student in each line came up to the RI and got into position, and once the students at all fifteen stations were ready, an RI with a megaphone said, "Ready. Set. Go."

The RIs at each station counted each student's correctly performed repetitions out loud. Two minutes later, the RI with the megaphone called "Stop!" ending the evaluation. Students who finished the minimum number of push-ups required for the event moved on to the next evaluation: sit-ups. Those who didn't complete the required number went to the back of the same line and retested once they returned to the front. That process continued until every student in the class completed their push-up and sit-up evaluations.

As instructed, I got in Sergeant Ferris's line. He looked at me as the line formed and tapped his watch with his index finger, taunting me, clearly trying to get in my head. It didn't work. *Go ahead. Doubt me, asshole.*

Finally, after about ten other students had completed their evaluation, I was at the front of the line.

"You excited to tell your friends about the one day you spent at ranger school, Air Force?" Sergeant Ferris asked.

"Negative, sergeant," I replied as I got into position and prepared to begin. *Just play the game.*

"Okay. Let's see what you got." Again with the big grin.

The RI timing the evaluations said over the megaphone, "Ready. Set. Go."

I was knocking out my push-ups quickly and with perfect form, back straight, chest almost touching the ground at the bottom, and locking out my elbows at the top.

Sergeant Ferris counted my repetitions out loud. "Thirty-eight,

Five Million Steps **147**

thirty-nine, forty."

*Nine more to go.*

"Forty-one, forty-one, forty-one, forty-one, all the way down, Air Force. Forty-one, forty-one, forty-one. Stop! You're a no-go, Air Force, get to the back of the line and try again."

*Are you fucking kidding me?* I was furious. He was still playing games with me, and there was nothing I could do about it. *Slow and steady on the next one. Don't let him get in your head. You've got this.*

Back at the front of the line again: "Those last ones were ugly. I don't think you've got forty-nine in you, Air Force."

"I'm good, sergeant."

"I doubt that."

"Ready. Set. Go."

That time I went slow and steady, still perfect form, quick pause at the bottom, quick pause at the top.

That time he let me finish. "Forty-seven, forty-eight, forty-nine, stop. You're a go, Air Force. Come see me again for sit-ups."

He pulled the same stunt with my sit-ups, making me do them twice, counting them properly on the second round. His games with me were over at that point, though. He couldn't touch me on my run evaluation. Everyone started at the same time, and those who made it across the finish line in under the time limit passed. Those who didn't failed. I came across the finish line with plenty of time to spare.

A different RI evaluated me on my chin-ups, and I passed those with no problem too. Sergeant Farris was an instructor for a different company than mine, so I was out of his immediate reach for the rest of the time I was at Fort Benning. We saw each other a few times in passing, though, and he gave me that same stupid grin every time.

Things went well for me during my remaining three weeks in that phase. I passed all my evaluations and graded patrols. All my time and experiences from pre-ranger were paying off. Over half my class quit and went home or failed something and were recycled into the class behind us. The rest of us moved on to the next phase of ranger school: the mountain phase.

The mountain phase is at Camp Merrill, near Dahlonega, Georgia, in the Tennessee Valley Divide. It was tougher than the Benning phase. We learned more advanced tactics, patrolling techniques, and military mountaineering. We were grouped into larger elements too, going from squads of eight to twelve students to platoons of about forty. The operations we conducted became more complex, as did our evaluations. The terrain and weather were much more difficult as well. I went through what is considered a "winter class" and was in the mountain phase from late November to mid-December.

We were three days away from finishing, and I was doing well. We'd be going home for ten days over Christmas before heading to the last phase of school, the swamp phase in Florida. I had passed all my patrols and was helping my classmates pass theirs as our time there came to an end. We had just finished planning and briefing our mission for the day and were starting our movement through the mountains.

We were in a heavily wooded area, and the temperature had dropped below freezing during the night. The ground and trees were covered with a light layer of frost. I stepped on a small fallen tree, slipped on the frost, and fell to my side. I stuck out my left arm to catch myself, a poor decision since I was wearing a pack that weighed nearly a hundred pounds. I felt a sharp pain in my wrist when my hand hit the ground, and I knew something wasn't right. I grabbed my wrist with my other hand, waiting for more pain, but there was none. Holding my hand in front of my face and rotating my thumb outward, I saw nothing out of the ordinary. *It doesn't look broken. Must not be too bad.* Holding my forearm still and rotating my wrist in a circle was a different story. I felt another sharp pain inside my wrist, near the base of my thumb. *Shit. Please tell me this thing isn't broken!*

Five Million Steps **149**

Coincidentally, one of the RIs was standing nearby when I fell and saw the whole thing. "You okay, ranger?" he asked as he walked toward me.

"I'm good, sergeant. I think I hurt my wrist, but it doesn't look broken."

By that point, he was standing over me. "Stand up, and let me see your wrist."

Leaving my pack on the ground, I slowly got up, using my right arm to help me while protecting my left. "See? Looks good, sergeant," I said, pulling up my sleeve and rolling my wrist around slightly.

"You busted your ass pretty good, ranger, and you're shaking right now. We're going to get you checked out."

He was right. I was shaking. I don't know if it was my nerves, the cold, or if it was from my injury, but I couldn't hold my hands still. *If this thing is broken, they're going to send me home. And I don't want to have to come back after getting this far.* I was almost two-thirds of the way through ranger school. If I was sent home, it would be months before I would heal and be able to come back to start a new class.

The medical team that came to check on us every morning hadn't left yet. They were loaded up in their ambulance on a nearby road, about to depart. The RI told them over the radio to wait and walked me down to the road to meet them. One of the medics checked me out, tested the range of motion in my wrist, and pushed his thumb directly on the spot that hurt the most. It was hard to hold still—it was really starting to hurt at that point.

"Probably a scaphoid fracture, but we can't be sure without an X-ray. We'll take him downtown to get him looked at," the medic told the RI.

"Thanks, guys," the RI said before telling me, "keep your head up, ranger, and get your ass back out here soon."

"Roger that, sergeant," I replied with a fake smile. Inside I was crushed. I had trained and prepared for over six years, more than half of my career, to get to ranger school. And now, I might be going home because I pulled a dumbass move and injured my wrist.

The rest of the morning was spent driving to a hospital in the nearby town to get my wrist x-rayed. The doctors there confirmed I had fractured my scaphoid and gave me a cast that covered my forearm, wrist, and thumb, but left my fingers exposed. The doctor told me I would have to wear the cast for two to three months. My hopes of finishing ranger school continued to dwindle.

Then it was back to Camp Merrill, where I awaited my fate. It was the battalion commander's decision whether I stayed in the course or got sent home. There was another injured student in the camp's clinic when I arrived. He had also slipped on frost that morning and received a small puncture wound to his calf from a broken tree limb that impaled him when he fell. He had already been treated when I arrived, received three stitches, and was also waiting for the battalion commander's decision.

I hadn't been waiting for more than five minutes when, to our surprise, the commander came to see us in person. He approached me first.

"What happened to you, ranger?" he asked.

I explained everything in detail and answered a few questions before he asked, "Well, what do you want to do?"

After intentionally leaving out the details about how long I would have to wear my cast, I said, "Stay and train, sir. This will probably heal over Christmas break, and I'm sure I'll be good to go for Florida." He knew I had already passed all my patrols, and I was essentially just doing time until the phase ended. In three days, I would never see him again.

"I get what you're saying, Air Force, but we're probably going to send you home. You can get healthy and come back again," he said, then went to check on the other injured student.

Those were the words I knew were coming but didn't want to hear. My frustration turned to sadness and disappointment.

Through the curtain separating our two beds in the clinic, I heard some of the conversation between the commander and the other injured student.

"What do you want to do?" the commander asked.

"I want to go home and come back when my leg heals," said the student.

The commander, clearly disappointed in his answer, shouted, "So you mean to tell me that you have three stitches and want to go home, while I have an air force guy next to you who broke his wrist and still wants to stay. Roger that, ranger. You're going to the house!"

I heard the curtain whip shut and footsteps fast approaching before my curtain flew open, the commander stuck his head in, and he said, "You're a go, Air Force. You're staying. I don't know what they're going to tell you in Florida, but I'm letting you finish the mountains."

I jumped up, completely surprised and ecstatic. "Thank you, sir! You won't regret this!"

It was such a relief to know I wasn't getting sent home. I would just have to figure out how to make it through the last phase without anyone knowing about my injury.

The last three days of the mountain phase went smoothly. I returned to the field to join my platoon after wrapping my arm in a black trash bag and taping it up to protect my cast from the weather. I got a lot of questions and laughs from the RIs and the other students too. It gave me a chance to throw some service rivalry jabs back at my army classmates. "You wouldn't see an army guy come back out here with a broken wrist!" always got them riled up. It was all in good fun, though, and they respected me for continuing despite my injury. And before I knew it, my class was done with the mountain phase of ranger school. Less than 100 of us remained of the more than 350 that started. I felt excited and lucky to be one of them.

The ten-day Christmas break flew by. During the break, I removed my cast and tried to keep my mobility and range of motion in my wrist while my good friend, ibuprofen, helped me manage the swelling and pain. Before I knew it, I was back at Fort Benning, reuniting with my class, picking up our gear, and loading on buses for the five-hour drive to Camp Rudder, the swamp phase, on Eglin Air Force Base, Florida.

When our buses pulled up at Camp Rudder, we found all the instructors waiting for us outside the buildings. It was time for ranger games again after being away for ten days. Our new crew of RIs welcomed us with an hour-long "scuff session" full of running, calisthenics, carrying each other on our backs, and crawling and rolling around in the grass, sand, and mud, all to remind us that we were back at ranger school and the instructors had missed us. It was like a late Christmas gift.

And the whole time, my wrist was killing me. We weren't allowed to use over-the-counter medicines, and I hadn't taken any ibuprofen since returning to Fort Benning two days before. Any time I put pressure on my wrist when it was bent, it caused excruciating pain. I figured out, though, that if I kept my wrist straight and put my fist on the ground instead of my open hand, it didn't hurt as much. None of the instructors noticed what I was doing, and it appeared that none of them even knew about my injury. I was safe, or so I thought.

Training continued, and I got used to dealing with my injured wrist. On the morning of the third day, my roster number was called by one of the RIs during our morning formation. "Roster number one-two-four, fall out and go see the medics."

*Aw shit, they found out about my wrist.*

I didn't know it at the time, but a folder was maintained for each student with all their information in it: their personal information, medical clearance paperwork, fitness assessment scores, evaluation forms, and notes on every interaction with school staff, including the medics. That folder traveled from phase to phase as the students made their way through the course.

I was greeted by an army physician's assistant (PA) at the clinic. I noticed he was also a ranger graduate and had a 1st Ranger Battalion combat patch on his right shoulder, signifying that he had been deployed in combat with that unit. *All right, this guy's probably gonna be cool about this.*

Five Million Steps    **153**

"So, air force, it says here that you got a scaphoid fracture in the mountains, but they let you stay. Is that true?" the PA asked me.

"Yes, sir, it is."

"It also says you got a cast, which was supposed to be on for two to three months. Is that true?"

"Yes, sir, it is."

With a clenched jaw, he asked, "Well, where's your fucking cast, ranger, and why haven't you told anyone about your wrist? You shouldn't even be here."

*So much for being cool about this.*

"I understand, sir, and I'm sorry for not saying anything. I took off my cast during the break. My wrist is fine now. I know I should have said something, but I'm just trying to make it through. I don't want to start over."

"Let me see your wrist, ranger."

I held it out in front of me, and after looking at it and lightly manipulating my wrist, he let go and said, "Hold them both out now and give me full range of motion and full rotations of both wrists, ranger. And keep going until I tell you to stop."

The pain was excruciating when I maxed out the range of motion on my left wrist. I did my best not to wince, shake, or show any signs that the movements were hurting me. The PA watched me move both wrists, the left obviously less smooth than the right, and he asked, "Does that hurt, ranger?"

"No, sir, it's good to go."

He stepped back, inhaled deeply, and held his breath for a moment before slowly exhaling. His face relaxed, and he said, "All right, ranger, check it out. I know you're full of shit and I know your wrist hurts, but I understand what you're trying to do, and I admire that. I'm going to let you continue training, but if I see you in here again, for anything, you're gone. You understand?"

Surprised and elated, I yelled, "Yes, sir, I do. Thank you so much. You won't see me again!" And I was out of there, back to training, never to return.

**154** Jason France

Three weeks later, I graduated from ranger school and pinned on my ranger tab. There were 130 students who graduated in my class. Of that number, only seventy were from the original group of over 350. The first two airmen graduated from ranger school in 1955, and I was the 136th airman in the school's history to graduate. The feeling of pride and accomplishment I had was too great to put into words. During the six years I spent pursuing my goal, I had overcome three significant injuries, attended pre-ranger four times, struggled with long periods of self-doubt and the doubt of leaders and peers in my organizations, and had to go above and beyond to prove that this airman had what it took to graduate the army's premier combat leadership school. And in the end, every part of the struggle was worth it.

CHAPTER 14

# PUTTING MYSELF FIRST

One of the most fulfilling experiences of my PCT journey was hiking through Goat Rocks Wilderness in Washington. There's a stretch of trail about two and a half miles long called the Knife's Edge. Its views, elevation, and narrow trail with sheer drop-offs on both sides make negotiating the edge one of the most memorable portions of the trail for most hikers. It certainly was for me.

I had planned on hiking over Cispus Pass, continuing six more miles, and reaching the Knife's Edge just before sunset. I had seen beautiful photos of that area during sunset, and I was hoping to have that experience and capture some images too.

The weather worsened as the day progressed, and it started pouring rain on me less than a mile from the first climb toward the edge. I decided to stop and set up camp since the rain had made the trail a muddy, slippery mess. I knew frozen snowfields were ahead in my path, some on very steep sections, and the rainfall could create potentially hazardous conditions. The rain and low clouds would have also prevented me from seeing the sunset. I was hopeful the storm would pass during the night, and I would wake up to clear skies and catch the sunrise instead.

I set up my camp in the pouring rain, cooked and ate my dinner inside my tent, prepared my gear so I could get out of camp quickly the next morning, and set my alarm for 4:30 a.m. I don't even remember falling asleep. It had been a long and strenuous few days.

It was still raining when my alarm went off, and the wind had picked up overnight. I peeked out of my tent and saw gray skies all around me. I set my alarm for five thirty and went back to sleep. When my alarm woke me the second time, the rain had stopped, but the wind still knocked my tent around. Thinking maybe at least the visibility had improved, I stuck my head out again, only to see that the conditions were still nowhere near what I'd hoped they would be.

I had been waiting for this day since I was a kid. This was where some of the photos in the *National Geographic* magazine were taken, the ones that sparked my desire to hike the PCT. I wanted clear skies so I could see Mount Rainier and the surrounding mountains of the Cascade Range for miles in all directions. I wanted to see the trail in front of me, take in the full scale of the climbs I would face, and get the feeling in my gut and the voice in my head telling me, *I'm about to get my ass kicked, but it's gonna be awesome!* I also wanted to see that trail behind me so I could fully appreciate the progress I was making. I wanted no wind so I could hear my footsteps and my breath, to keep my eyes up and drink in the views instead of getting tossed around, being forced to keep my gaze on the ground, focusing on the trail with every step, and worrying about the sheer drop-offs—many going hundreds of feet straight down. I wanted the experience to measure up to the image of perfection I had created in my mind for over forty years.

I knew that image of perfection wouldn't become a reality that day, but I still had the opportunity to create a new one. The rewards I received through facing uncertainty on my journey were some of the most significant rewards of my life, and this would turn out to be another one of those great rewards. And the best thing about it was I didn't do it for anyone but myself, something I hadn't done in a very long time.

• • •

Integrity first, service before self, and excellence in all we do—those are the three core values of the United States Air Force. They were made official in 1995, five years after I had enlisted, and I lived by those core values for the rest of my career. They guided me and gave me purpose as an airman. The first and the last one was easy. The second one, though, was a bit complicated. The intent behind the core value of service before self is to reinforce that, as an airman, duty comes before personal desires. It's about discipline, self-control, and respect—not implying that the air force comes before everything else in your life, though.

That's sometimes easier said than done, though, especially the longer someone serves. As I progressed through my career, serving in positions of increased responsibility and larger organizations, the expectations and demands also increased, and the lines blurred. I allowed service before self to turn into service over self, service instead of self, and sometimes service and *no* self. And I let my focus of taking care of other people to sometimes come at the expense of my own self-care.

Also, as I progressed, my world became more complicated. The projects I led and worked on, and the problems I had to solve, became more complex. The higher workload meant less margin and flexibility in my schedule. Managing my time became more difficult, and my days were often a series of fifteen-minute increments from the time I came in until the time I left for the day. I had to be selective about what I took on, what I didn't take on, and what I delegated to someone else. But I was still a chief, and my main focus always remained on taking care of what was most important: people. And with that, if someone showed up truly needing my help, I would stop what

I was doing, and the focus would shift to them. Whatever I was working on could be dealt with later. Taking care of people was what I loved most about my job, and the greatest reward for me was to help others succeed, even when it was at my own expense.

Some of my predicament was self-imposed, though. I had built a reputation for getting things done and helping people succeed, which felt good. I had an image to uphold as a chief, one who truly cares about his people and shows it through actions, not words. And I took great pride in my ability to "get it all done" despite the difficulty or the personal toll it took on me.

I took it too far without fully realizing it. Doing something for myself often ended up being a day of personal leave to get work done at home so I could catch up or focus without the distractions I faced in the office. Sometimes it was taking a week off to do something with my family but still being tied to my devices and doing thirty minutes of work each morning and evening so I wouldn't be buried with work when I returned. I even sold forty-five days of leave back to the air force over my career instead of using it for myself. And for the last few years of my career, I would rush to burn my annual leave before the fiscal year ended so I wouldn't lose it, usually doing work at home on those days.

All those choices were mine, though, and I own them all. I could have retired at any time during my last eleven years in the air force. I probably could have gotten away with letting some things slip, referred some of the people who needed my help to someone else, or maybe refused to let anything impact my schedule or time away from work, but that wasn't who I was.

After finishing a career of selfless service, I needed to do something meaningful for myself, something big, and the PCT was precisely that. I needed something that would bring out the best version of myself, something I had always worked hard to be as a husband, father, and airman but neglected with regard to myself as an individual. I needed to do something where I had to rely only on myself.

**160** Jason France

For years I had been prepared, briefed, watched after, and lifted by the incredible people who cared about and surrounded me. I appreciated everything people poured into me, but I needed to do something completely on my own. I needed to risk failing at something big that didn't have a high probability of success, something that not many people can endure and complete. My career had become easy in the sense that I would've had to do something monumental to fail. I needed to feel the excitement of uncertainty again. Most things toward the end of my career were predictable; I usually saw the outcomes way before what I was working on was complete. I needed to face something I couldn't see far enough to know how it would end, or what the next day would bring. And finally, I needed to get out of my comfort zone, to explore and challenge myself in a new way, bigger than I ever had before. My biggest rewards in life have always come after the most challenging and uncomfortable situations.

I got all those things and more during my PCT journey. Doing something for myself felt strange and uncomfortable at first, though. I felt guilty too, asking myself what kind of husband and father leaves his family to hike alone for five months. But they supported me fully, and I returned as a better husband and father for the experience.

Once I overcame the uncomfortable feelings, I enjoyed the freedom I had never experienced. I was twelve when I got my first job, delivering newspapers, and kept working until retiring from the air force, nearly thirty-seven years later. I had never experienced the freedom I did on the PCT. I set the terms instead of doing things on someone else's. I didn't have to ask for permission. I didn't have to force my experience into a certain number of days. I didn't have to accommodate someone else's needs, wasn't responsible for anyone else, and wasn't concerned about their experience or thoughts. And I didn't have to drop what I was doing for someone else at a moment's notice. I could be genuinely present for myself and no one else for the first time.

Five Million Steps   **161**

· · ·

The cloud ceiling dropped as I broke camp, and I was inside the clouds as I approached the Knife's Edge. The visibility was poor, with nothing but bright-white haze all around. I could only see a few hundred feet around me, but the view of the trail before me was clear and allowed me to navigate the wet and slippery mess. Through the mist I could see cairns in the distance—large piles of rocks, some five feet tall, that help hikers navigate in conditions like I was experiencing. Continuing my climb, the trail turned from dirt and mud to rocks that, although no longer muddy, were just as slippery and more difficult to walk on. The conditions worsened as I continued, both the weather and the trail. I thought about turning back and waiting a few hours for the weather to clear, but I was already committed and embracing the suck to the fullest.

The further I went, the more the suck turned into excitement. The wind was blowing all around me and was so loud in some areas that I couldn't hear myself think. The trail that ran along the Knife's Edge was like a roller coaster: big climbs, narrow trail with sheer drop-offs on both sides along the high points, and back down before the next part of the ride. The higher I went, the thinner the clouds were. The sun kept peeking through, and I caught glimpses of the top of Mount Rainier in the distance, surrounded by a blanket of clouds, before it disappeared from my view again. The clouds were rushing over the ridges in front of me, also pushed by the intense wind. I was wet from the mist of the clouds, my hands were numb, my face stung, and my eyes were watering. It was exhilarating. There is nothing in my life I can compare that experience with; it gave me a new image of perfection in my mind. I felt more alive running along Knife's Edge than I can ever remember, and I did it all for myself.

# CHAPTER 15

# EVOLUTION

I caught my first close-up view of Mount Rainier while traversing the Knife's Edge. I had hiked almost twenty-three hundred miles for that view, which made me think of all that had changed since my first hike in Olympic National Park when I was nine. My hiking experiences as a kid built the foundation of my outdoor skills and passion for hiking. However, it wasn't until 2003, when I hiked the ninety-three-mile Wonderland Trail, which circumnavigates Mount Rainier, that I had an actual immersive solo hiking experience. Seeing Mount Rainier again reminded me of the mistakes I'd made on my Wonderland Trail hike and how I'd leveraged those mistakes and evolved into the hiker I am today.

The first two words that come to mind when I reflect on my Wonderland Trail adventure are misery and growth: misery in many aspects of the hike, but growth from the experience. The two most significant sources of misery were my poor choices of equipment and my poor planning. I wore hiking boots that weighed close to three pounds, about the same as those I wore at work. They were heavy and impractical for hiking, but they felt comfortable right out of the box and were expensive, so I figured I would be fine without breaking them in. The first mile I put on them was on the Wonderland.

**163**

I bought an Osprey Crescent 110 expedition pack for the hike. The pack alone weighed seven and a half pounds and had a 110-liter capacity. It had comfortable straps and a waist belt, luxurious compared with the military rucksack I had been using for years. The first mile I put on it was on the trail, just like my boots. Of course, 110 liters of capacity meant I had to fill all 110 liters with stuff. I carried a pair of running shoes to use as camp shoes. I packed a pair of Teva sandals I never wore; I thought I should bring them because of articles, advertisements, and photos I saw in magazines. I carried a water filter that weighed over a pound. I bought it because it was the most expensive filter at REI, so I figured it had to be the best. I carried three eight-ounce canisters of fuel, never calculating how much I would need for an eight-day hike. There was also a three-piece aluminum pot set, six pairs of socks and underwear, four T-shirts, three pairs of shorts, and a five-pound sleeping bag. I weighed the pack at a ranger station right before stepping onto the trail. It was over sixty pounds. At the time I wondered, *Why did all the rangers come out to see me weigh this thing?*

I hadn't planned for how much food I would need, how much fuel I would use, the distance between water sources, how the elevation changes would affect my pace and mileage, or the impacts of traveling over miles of snow. I made countless planning oversights. Those oversights led to many mistakes, but more importantly, to a lot of learning and growth.

So, after ninety-three miles of blisters, frustration, embarrassment, and pain in places I didn't know could hurt, I walked away humbled, better for the experience, and eager to improve and get back on the trail. When I got home, I replaced most of my gear with lighter, more functional items. I reduced my kit to only what I needed, and nothing more. I thoroughly tested everything, and if it didn't work exactly the way I needed it to, I sold it, got something new, and tried again. I made no compromises until I found exactly what matched my needs and hiking style. My experiences on the Wonderland

**164** Jason France

Trail started my evolution as a hiker, an evolution that will never end as I learn and grow from every hiking experience.

My close-up view of Mount Rainier allowed me to see how it had also changed over the eighteen years since I'd hiked the Wonderland Trail. Although still beautiful, the years of melting glaciers, landslides, rockfalls, and floods had changed its appearance. Sections of trail had been destroyed in those events, but new trails had since been constructed, giving people new opportunities to explore its beauty.

Lost in my thoughts as I took in the amazing views of the "new" Mount Rainier, I couldn't help but think about my evolution in my personal life and career. Of all the ways I've evolved and matured in life, recovering from addiction to alcohol as a teenager was one of the hardest yet most important changes I've ever made.

I started drinking the day I turned fifteen. My mother gave me a six-pack of beer and a pizza for my birthday. I got drunk that night. I liked how it made me feel and the escape it gave me. It only took that one time for me to get hooked, and I wanted to get that feeling as often as I could. I was too young to realize it at the time, but my introduction to drinking came at a very vulnerable period in my life. I was never diagnosed as an addict, but I'd be surprised if I weren't. Addiction runs in my family: alcohol, drugs, excessive behaviors, and abusive relationships. I had seen the toll that addiction had taken on many of my relatives but wasn't mature enough to understand how quickly it started to take a toll on me.

Soon it took more beer to give me the buzz I was looking for, and before I knew it, I'd progressed to hard liquor. Alcohol was never hard for me to get ahold of, whether it was a can or two of beer from the refrigerator at a friend's house or a quick swig from a bottle in their parents' liquor cabinet. Getting my driver's license didn't stop or even deter me from drinking. It made it easier for me since having a car gave me more options of places to get alcohol and drink away from home. I have no idea how many times I

Five Million Steps **165**

drove drunk, how many lives I put in danger, or how many close calls there were. There were many mornings—and in many cases afternoons—when I would wake up not knowing how I made it home. I would get up and see my car outside but couldn't remember driving it home.

My typical night of drinking started in a liquor store or convenience store parking lot. I would hang out there, wait for someone who looked friendly to get out of their car, and ask them to buy me a six-pack or a bottle. It never took long. Some even told me to be careful and have fun after they gave me a bottle. There was a navy base in the town where I grew up too. Young sailors who were of legal age and remembered what it was like to be in high school and want a good time were usually the easiest targets. There were also friends from work who were old enough to buy alcohol, friends with siblings who were old enough, and friends who would steal liquor from their parents. I didn't care where I got it, as long as I did. Some of the other kids I hung around drank too.

When I was going to drink with friends, I would start before we got together whenever I could. Even though they were my friends, and I got alcohol from them sometimes, I didn't want them to know how much I drank. And sadly, I also wanted more for myself. If I had told them I had started before we met up, it might have meant getting less of the share of what we scored together. I got good at hiding my drinking, and I got good at hiding my other problems too. But instead of feeling good about my ability to hide things, I felt guilty for deceiving people. I knew what I was doing was wrong, but so long as I got that buzz, I didn't care enough to stop. And no one noticed until it was almost too late.

I enlisted in the air force a month before I graduated high school, but I had to wait nine months before I went to basic training. I spent those nine months working, hanging out with my friends from high school, and drinking nearly every night.

One night I spent a couple of hours parked at a remote beach near my house. I had been there many times before and knew not many people, including the police, passed by very often. It was one of my favorite spots to drink alone. I had already chugged a forty-ounce bottle, a "forty," of malt liquor that I had talked someone into buying for me at a convenience store earlier that day. I didn't have much of a buzz—it was still early—and I wanted more beer, so I drove back to the same store to try to score my next round.

I parked my car on the side of the store, around the corner from the front entrance and windows, just like I had done so many times before. A car pulled up. The driver was an older lady, not my typical target, but she looked friendly. I jumped out and walked quickly toward her, hoping to catch her before she went inside.

"Excuse me, ma'am," I said just before she reached the sidewalk in front of the store.

Startled by my sudden presence, she froze, looking at me with wide eyes and raised eyebrows. I smiled reassuringly. "Hello, ma'am. If I give you ten bucks, could I trouble you to buy me some beer for my dad?"

She frowned. "Why can't he buy it himself?"

"He's working late," I said calmly. "I want to surprise him when he gets home."

Her frown deepened, and she snapped, "No. Absolutely not." She rushed into the store.

I went back to my car. A second car pulled up, a navy guy, still in uniform. Same thing, I asked if he could buy me some beer for my dad. He knew I was lying and told me, "Hell, no! I'm not going down for buying beer for some kid." So back to my car I went to wait for the next car to pull up.

Parking on the side of the store prevented the people inside, including the cashier, from seeing what I was doing. But it also prevented me from seeing what *they* were doing. One of the people I approached—not sure if it was the lady or the navy guy—told the cashier that I was outside and had asked them to buy beer for me. The cashier called the police. I had no

Five Million Steps **167**

idea. I watched both people drive away after they came out of the store and didn't suspect anything.

I dozed off while waiting for the next car to show up and didn't notice a police car pull up and the officer go inside. I was awakened by a tapping on my side window and a bright light shining in my face. I knew immediately it was a cop. My car was running so I could have the heat on, I was the only one inside, and I had been drinking. It didn't matter that I probably wasn't legally drunk; I was still under twenty-one, and I knew I was in a lot of trouble.

There was no hiding the fact that I had been drinking. I had a hard time answering the questions he threw at me as I gave him my license and registration, and before I knew it, I was in handcuffs in the back of his car. I was leaving for basic training in less than two months, and all I could think about was losing the only option I had to make something of myself, and the only chance I felt I had to get away from home.

I didn't realize it at first because I was buzzed and nervous, but I had met the cop before, and he recognized me.

"Aren't you the kid who works in the produce department at Safeway?" he asked.

"Yes, sir."

"And didn't you tell me you're going into the air force to be a security policeman?"

I remembered him as soon as he asked. He had come into the store in uniform a few weeks earlier. I had asked him what it was like being a cop and told him I was going into the air force to be a cop too. We talked for a long time in the store that day. He told me stories about the things he had done and seen. It was exciting to hear, and he was excited for me too. He congratulated me and wished me the best before leaving. And here I was, in handcuffs in the back of his police car for who-knew-how-many alcohol-related offenses.

"Yes, sir. That was me," I said quietly, my head down.

"This is not the way to prepare for a career in law enforcement, Jason. We don't need people like you in this line of work."

That hurt to hear, but I deserved it. "Yes, sir. I know."

"I'll be back in a minute. Don't do anything stupid in the back of my car," he said before returning to the store.

*Pretty sure I've done enough stupid shit for tonight.*

He and I both knew that whatever decision he was about to make would dictate how the rest of my life would go. I thought I was going to jail and that my opportunity to join the air force, the one chance I had for a better future, was gone. I was scared. I was disappointed in myself. I felt helpless. I felt more alone than I ever had. All I could do was sit in the back of the police car and cry.

After what seemed like hours, he came around the corner with a cup of coffee in each hand. Embarrassed that I was crying, I wiped my eyes with my shirt sleeves as he approached. He carefully set the cups of coffee on the roof, opened my door, and told me to get out.

"Put out your hands so I can take the cuffs off, Jason."

"Yes, sir," I said with surprise, holding out my hands.

He took off the cuffs. "Get whatever you need out of your car and lock it up. I'm taking you home. Sit in the front."

*Holy shit! Is this guy really going to let me off?*

I didn't say a word. I just did what I was told. I got my jacket and wallet, locked my car, and got in the front seat of his. Whatever buzz I'd had was almost gone, and I was beginning to regain my clarity.

As I got in the car, he handed me one of the cups of coffee and said sternly, "Here, drink this and get your shit together. We've got a lot to talk about, and I need you to remember it." As stern as his voice was, his look was different since coming out of the store.

The ten-minute drive to my house took almost an hour. He told me how disappointed he was in me. He told me I was better than that. He told me I could have a bright future ahead. He told me I would throw it all away if I didn't change and start making better choices. And he told me about the horrible things he had seen because of people driving drunk. No one had ever spoken to me in such a powerful and meaningful way. He gave me a talk a father would have given me.

The last thing he shared was a similar mistake he'd made as a young man, a mistake that nearly cost him the opportunity to become a police officer, and nearly cost someone their life. He got choked up. I was sobbing again. The experience hit us both deeply. I was appreciative, not only because he let me go but because he cared and told me the things I needed to hear that I don't believe anyone else would have.

He dropped me off around the corner from my house so no one would see me getting out of a police car. The last thing he said to me was, "Remember everything that happened tonight, Jason. You've got to change, and you're the only one who can make that happen. This might be your only chance. Don't waste it."

That experience is still with me. I wish I could say I quit drinking for good that night, but I didn't. He gave me the push I needed to start, though. Six weeks of Air Force Basic Military Training, with no access to alcohol, and four months of technical training were helpful too. There were still a few periods in my life afterward when I drank a lot, but after a few more years of ups and downs in my relationship with alcohol, I evolved and got to a place where I regained, and have since maintained, my control and ability to choose.

Countless events contributed to my evolution throughout my thirty-one-year career in the air force too. One of the most impactful was at the beginning of my career, when I was almost forced to separate after my first enlistment.

I was a prideful young airman. I felt a great sense of accomplishment after graduating basic and technical training. My confidence grew as time passed, and I gained knowledge, skills, and experience as a security policeman. I became very good at my job but failed to realize that skill alone didn't make me a good airman. My confidence quickly turned into cockiness, and I developed a selfish attitude, putting what was important to me before anything and anyone else. My selfishness showed the most when working with other people. Despite overcoming my struggles growing up, I failed to use those experiences to help others around me. I adopted a "survival of the fittest" mindset and viewed someone else's struggles as a sign of weakness. *I had it harder than you, and I was still able to push through. Why can't you?* I separated myself from people and situations where I could have helped instead of leaning in and supporting them. My supervisors noticed this, and my annual evaluations—Enlisted Performance Reports (EPRs)—showed it. I was consistently marked down in the areas of "communicating with others" and "fostering teamwork." I didn't take the advice of my supervisors when they told me I needed to improve in those areas, and I didn't take the ratings on my EPRs seriously. I thought I was untouchable.

In the summer of 1993, approaching the end of my first four-year enlistment in the air force, I entered the window for possible reenlistment. At the time, the air force didn't face the recruitment and retention challenges they have faced in recent years. It was quite the opposite. We had too many people in some career fields, mine included, and only the best airmen were allowed to reenlist.

The air force used a program called Career Job Reservation (CJR) to manage the number of airmen on their first term of enlistment who were allowed to reenlist in overmanned career fields. If your CJR was approved, you reenlisted in your career field. If it was rejected, you had to separate or retrain into an undermanned career field if you met the requirements to enter that field.

Our EPRs were some of the tools used to determine which airmen would be awarded a CJR. At the time, enlisted airmen were rated on a one-to-five scale on their EPRs, with five being the best. The three most recent EPRs determined my rank order among the other airmen competing for a CJR in the same window as me. Most airmen in my career had received fives on all three of their EPRs. Some had two fives and one four. I had only one five and two fours, putting me far enough down the list that I didn't make the cut and was ineligible to reenlist in security police.

The only option I had was to retrain into a different field. I wanted to challenge myself in new ways and was eager to try one of the undermanned career fields anyway, so this presented an opportunity for me to stay in the air force and move to a job that I believed would be more fulfilling. It seemed like a win-win situation for me and the air force, so I took it and was accepted to retrain. They required me to extend my original enlistment contract by two years, which I did happily. However, shortly after my extension was approved, my retrain was erroneously canceled.

I went from the high of getting to stay in the air force and move to a new career field to the absolute low of thinking I was going to get kicked out. I was on pins and needles for two weeks before everything got sorted out and I received the final outcome. Since my enlistment extension had already been approved—even though it was technically for a different career field—it created a loophole that prevented me from having to separate. I was allowed to stay in the air force, still in security police, despite my CJR being denied.

I was lucky that I got to stay in. But I didn't take it for granted. It was the wake-up call I needed to get my bad attitude in check, learn to appreciate the amazing people I had the privilege to serve with, use my struggles and experiences to help others, and commit to a life of service instead of selfishness. And that's precisely what I did for the rest of my career.

I thought about that situation moments before I stepped on stage at my retirement ceremony. Part of me thought, *How did you make it this far? You're lucky even to be here.* But I also realized it was a necessary part of my evolution. It helped shape me into the airman I became.

What people saw of me on the Pacific Crest Trail wasn't just the result of over forty years of evolution as a hiker. It was the result of my evolution through all things in life.

CHAPTER 16

# SUCCESS

Washington was the most physically challenging state to hike through, and I worked harder there than any other section of the trail. Although it was lower in elevation than the Sierra Nevada mountain range, the daily ascents and descents were more demanding, the terrain was more challenging to navigate, and the weather varied more than in California and Oregon. One day I would have clear skies, the sun beating down on me, temperatures in the high eighties, and high humidity keeping me soaked in sweat. The next day it would be in the forties and pouring rain all day. I'd be wearing most of my clothes and constantly moving to stay warm. I'd set up camp with shaking, almost numb, hands and go to sleep damp and shivering.

Today was beautiful, though, with nearly perfect conditions for hiking. I broke camp and got on the trail earlier than usual. I needed to reach the High Bridge Ranger Station before three to catch the last National Park Service shuttle bus that would bring me into Stehekin. That was the last bus for the day, and missing it would have meant hiking an additional eleven miles, all on the road, to get to town. I also needed to get to the post office before it closed to pick up my last resupply box, and I wouldn't have been

**175**

able to hike twenty-nine miles and still make it in time.

Shortly after leaving camp, I crossed the point where I had less than a hundred miles left to reach the northern terminus. It was an exciting moment, and despite my mind telling me to pick up the pace, I took it slow. I remembered the feeling of accomplishment months ago when I reached the hundred-mile mark and everything I had experienced since. I maintained my easy pace all day, enjoying the spectacular mountain views in the morning before dropping in elevation and spending the rest of the day in the forest and pushing through the dense vegetation that covered the trail near the streams and rivers.

I knew I was getting close to my target when I entered Lake Chelan National Recreation Area, and less than two miles later, the boundary of North Cascades National Park, the last of the seven national parks I would hike through during my journey. Reaching the national park boundary also marked the last forest fire zone I had to worry about. Those were the first of many "lasts" I would experience in the days that followed. They were all signs that my journey was coming to an end.

Just before reaching the ranger station, I crossed the bridge that spans high above Agnes Creek. The water below was powerful and beautiful, a combination of whites, blues, and greens. I stood on the bridge for a few moments, closing my eyes and listening to the sound of the rushing water below, feeling the cool breeze on my face, and enjoying the smell of moist air and the surrounding trees. It was one of the countless moments of absolute contentment I experienced on my journey. I knew I would miss experiences like that. I would be off the trail soon, and they would be only memories. I could have stayed on the bridge for hours, but I had to enjoy the brief moment and keep moving.

I was the only hiker at the ranger station when I arrived at 2:30 p.m. It had been a short day mileage-wise; I had only hiked eighteen miles from last night's camp. I averaged around twenty-five miles a day through my home state, but it was nice to have a more relaxing day and finish early. I was excited to spend some time in the last town I would pass through before finishing my journey.

I explored the area, found the sign and pick-up point for the bus, took off my pack, and sat at one of the nearby picnic tables. I had eaten all but a few food items I'd carried since my last resupply 110 miles ago, and although my pack was lighter than usual, it felt great to take it off and relax on something other than the ground, a log, or a rock.

As soon as I took off my pack, the familiar but always unpleasant cold shock hit me when the breeze caught the sweat-soaked fabric on the back of my shirt. I shivered and felt goose bumps rise. After decades of hiking, I have never gotten used to that feeling.

Also familiar and unpleasant was the smell that hit me. I was sweaty and grimy from five days of hiking through the rugged Washington terrain while wearing the same shirt every day. It was covered in salt stains from being soaked with sweat and drying out repeatedly, and it smelled horrible.

It wasn't quite eye-watering, but it was bad enough for me to take it off and drape it over a rock near the picnic table so the sun and breeze could dry it out before the bus arrived. I put on the only other shirt in my pack, the T-shirt I wore in camp and to sleep in. I'm not sure why I cared that day, but I wanted to smell a little better on the bus ride to Stehekin. I think I was just tired of stinking all the time. I was ready to get to town, take a shower, wash my clothes, and get some rest before I got back on the trail for the final eighty-mile push to the Canadian border.

Other hikers started trickling in as I finished changing and organizing my things. They all had the same worn-down looks on their faces, all dirty from head to toe from the last stretch of trail, and all eager to get into town. Some sat at other picnic tables, some lay on the ground, some set down their packs, and others kept walking around so they wouldn't cramp up. Usually, when a group of hikers got together like that, there were stories, lots

Five Million Steps **177**

of laughter, photos, and a lot of energy all around. Not this time, though. It was oddly quiet, and I think we all had similar thoughts going through our minds: our time on the trail was coming to an end.

There were twelve of us waiting when the bus arrived. Happy but quiet, we paid the driver, loaded up, and found our seats. The ride to Stehekin was slow, bumpy, and dusty for the first few miles as we traveled on a dirt road. The energy of our group picked up as we got closer to town and started seeing signs of civilization. Soon we would have food, showers, and clean clothes. It also dawned on me that this would be my last ride in a vehicle until I was done with the trail and making my way home.

We rounded a corner, and there was the Pacific Crest Trail icon that we had all hiked almost twenty-six hundred miles to reach: the Stehekin Pastry Company. Everyone on the bus cheered as we pulled into the parking lot. A few of us were concerned that the delay would prevent us from making it to the post office before it closed, but the driver assured us we could make it as long as no one took too long in the bakery. We left our packs in our seats and dashed for the doors.

As soon as I entered, I saw that all the great things I had heard about the place were true. The employees were all welcoming, and they greeted us with smiles and congratulations. The smell was amazing, too, and triggered an indescribable hunger. I was consuming over five thousand calories a day at that point and was prepared to double that amount with what I was about to devour. Cinnamon rolls, sticky buns, muffins, cupcakes, cookies, pies, sandwiches, soup, salads, ice cream—it was almost overwhelming.

I bought four huge cinnamon rolls, four sticky buns, and four of what turned out to be my favorite pastry of all time and in all the world: the raspberry hazelnut roll. As I was at the register and my items were being boxed up and put in a bag, I added two more sticky buns to eat in the bakery and their biggest to-go cup of coffee.

Everyone made big orders. One hiker walked out with a large bag of pastries and two whole pies. I asked if he was buying extra to share with others, and his response was "No, bro, all for me."

I put down the two sticky buns in no time flat. Then, without a care in the world, I wiped my face and fingers with my shirt, knowing I would be doing laundry in an hour or two. Then it was back on the bus to finish the ride into town.

Stehekin, Washington, is a small community in the North Cascades that sits near the northern tip of Lake Chelan on the eastern shore. It has less than a hundred permanent residents and can only be accessed by foot, boat, seaplane, or helicopter. Most visitors get there on ferries that run from the town of Chelan, about fifty miles away on the lake's southern end. The community is comprised primarily of resorts, vacation homes, rental cabins, campgrounds, and small businesses that support the residents, seasonal workers, and the many vacationers and tourists who visit.

The bus driver dropped us off in the town center, where there was a lodge with a restaurant and a small convenience store. We were near the waterfront, and as I looked across the lake, I noticed a small amount of smoke that the wind had carried up from the forest fires burning to the south.

About a hundred tourists were walking around town when we pulled up. Being around so many people who weren't PCT hikers felt strange. They were all so clean and smelled good. My sense of smell had changed after being on the trail for so long. The scents of soap, shampoo, and laundry detergent were always stronger when I came off the trail. Most of the tourists were oblivious to us hikers, who had spent months on the trail to get there instead of the three-hour boat ride many of them had taken earlier that day. There were quite a few families with kids too. Seeing those families made me miss mine, and I was excited to know I would be home with them soon.

My first stop was the post office, where I picked up my final resupply box. It was the twenty-third resupply box of my hike. I had sent the five

Five Million Steps   **179**

packages I needed to get through Washington while I was in Portland, Oregon. The other four had brought me this far, and this last box would take me the final eighty miles to Canada and the thirty miles back to Harts Pass; entry into Canada was still prohibited due to the COVID-19 pandemic. There was also a possibility that I wouldn't be able to get a ride with someone driving back to town from Harts Pass. In that case, I'd have to camp there overnight and hike about twenty miles down the steep and winding dirt road that led to the town of Mazama.

This was one of the biggest resupply boxes of the entire trip. The number of calories I was burning every day was the highest of the whole journey, which meant I had to carry a lot more food than I did earlier on the trail. The colder temperatures in Northern Washington also made me burn more calories. The six-day food supply in that box would have easily lasted me more than ten days at the beginning of my hike.

Fitting everything into my pack was another challenge. I'd added some heavier insulating clothing before entering Washington. The additional weight wasn't much of a concern, but they took up more space inside my pack, which meant less room for food. Going over every item when planning food for each section was always tedious, but I was more critical of this resupply than any other. I needed food for full first breakfasts, full second breakfasts, morning snacks, lunches, afternoon snacks, dinners, and snacks to eat before bed. Multiply that by six, and add some cinnamon rolls and sticky buns, and it equaled more than my pack could hold.

I made a tough call, removed one day's worth of food (not the pastries!), donated it to another hiker, and hoped for the best. I figured if I ran out of food before I came off the trail, at least I would only be hungry for a day. Miraculously, I made it all fit after my last-minute changes.

Even though I got all the food in my pack, I wasn't looking forward to eating any of it. After months of eating the same things, I was sick of it. None of it tasted good to me anymore. I was ready to eat regular food again, to have options and the ability to change my mind on the spot if I wanted to. The freeze-dried meals, ramen, instant mashed potatoes, tuna and chicken packets, nutrition bars, tortillas, jerky, mixed nuts, nut butter packets, candy bars, instant oatmeal, instant coffee, and electrolyte powders had long lost their appeal. It wasn't just the taste I was tired of; the smells and textures also disgusted me. It was truly a matter of consuming food to fuel my body and nothing else. I was happy that soon I wouldn't have to force down any more unpleasant meals.

After getting my food situated, I took my last shower and did my last load of laundry. The main store in Stehekin sold shower and laundry "kits" consisting of quarters for the showers, washers, and dryers; a towel; and small containers of shampoo, soap, and laundry detergent. One small building housed both the shower and laundry rooms. It was down the street from the central part of town, away from the area busy with tourists. In true hiker trash fashion, I wrapped myself in the towel, threw my clothes into the washer, and started it. There were only nine items in total. Soon most of the simplicity I experienced on the PCT, including the few items of clothing I needed, would be gone, and I would be back in the "real world."

Still wrapped in a towel, I headed to the adjacent room to shower. That's when I was hit with another big sign that it was time to finish and get home. I looked at myself in the mirror and was surprised at what I saw. I hadn't paid much attention before when I saw myself in the mirror at hotels, hostels, or other places where I showered on the trail. Looking at myself closely from head to toe, I realized I looked like hell.

I didn't know exactly how much weight I had lost at the time (it turned out to be forty-three pounds), but it was a lot. Most of the muscle on my upper body was gone. I could see my ribs, clavicles, and hip bones protruding. My arms were the thinnest I ever remembered them being. My legs were strong from carrying me so far, but they were thin and only effective in the limited range of motion required to hike. Many people think you get

Five Million Steps **181**

in great shape from hiking for so long, but overall, I was in terrible shape. I had deep red-and-purple chafe marks that had turned into rough patches on my shoulders and lower back from my pack rubbing against my skin day in and day out. I had lost four toenails from kicking rocks and roots sticking up from the trail and from walking so many miles every day for months.

There were also ailments that weren't visible. Something on my body was hurting all the time, so much so that I forgot what it felt like to have no pain. My knees hurt so bad that they would wake me up every night, sometimes several times. I had plantar fasciitis in my right foot that stretching, massaging, or soaking in cold streams throughout the day didn't help. I had terrible Achilles tendinitis on both sides, and neither stretching nor mobility work alleviated it. I had a recurring quad strain I had been dealing with since early in the Sierra that always picked the worst time to return. And the three outside toes on both feet were numb from the constant pressure from walking so far every day with a heavy pack.

It took me forever to get up and moving most days. I was pumping ibuprofen and acetaminophen with my morning coffee and several times throughout the day to help reduce the pain and swelling in my legs and feet. I hobbled around camp every morning, wincing in pain, until I was mobile enough to put on my pack and hit the trail. Once I got moving, the endorphins kicked in, and the joy of being on the trail hit me. I felt great as long as I kept moving.

I also had to laugh at myself as I looked at my hair and beard in front of the mirror. My hair hadn't been that long since high school, and I had never grown a beard this long. Even though the five months of growth covered most of my features, I could still see how thin my face had become. I hadn't cut my hair or shaved at Justin's request. My family had only ever seen me with short hair and no real amount of facial hair before. When I was in the military and on leave, I only went a few days without shaving, and I rarely went more than two weeks between haircuts. So when my then-eleven-year-old son asked me to grow out my hair and beard, it was an easy yes.

After showering and finishing my laundry, I put on my freshly cleaned clothes and walked back to the lodge at the center of town. Several other hikers were gathered on the patio outside of the convenience store. I bought some snacks and sat alone at a table overlooking Lake Chelan, enjoying being clean, wearing clean clothes, and simply relaxing. Some of the other hikers were connected to the free but spotty Wi-Fi provided by the lodge and were arranging their trips home. Some chatted with their friends or families, and others just relaxed, not seeming to have a care in the world.

I made a FaceTime call to my family. It had been a week since I spoke with them, and I was excited to share that I had made it to Stehekin. The next time I saw their faces, I would be on my way home. The poor connection prevented us from talking long, but seeing the excitement on their faces warmed my heart. Here was another sign that it was time for me to finish and get home.

Still sitting on the patio, I watched the group of tourists that had spent the day in town load up and depart on the last ferry back to Chelan. They would all be back in their cars in less than three hours, and many would sleep in their beds that night. I still had 110 miles to hike, a long car ride to Seattle, and a plane ride to St. Louis, all taking over a week before I would be home and sleeping in my bed again.

Stehekin was a different place after the tourists left, and only a small number of hikers, residents, and people staying at the local lodges and vacation rentals remained. It was quiet and much more peaceful. Everything seemed to slow down too. Since I had finished all I needed to do before returning to the trail the following day, I started to think more about how close I was to the end.

I was zoned out, staring at the lake, when another hiker asked, "You ready to get this last bit knocked out and hit that terminus, Meat Grinder?"

Five Million Steps **183**

"Yes, I am, brother."

"Me too, man. Mother Nature has been telling us it's time to get off the trail before she starts kicking our ass."

He was right. I hadn't thought much about it until he mentioned it, but I started the hike in the spring, and now autumn was less than two weeks away. The fall colors were beginning to emerge in the trees, and the wildflowers were nearly gone. The days were getting shorter, the distances I covered during daylight hours were decreasing, and the sun wasn't waking me up as early anymore. The daytime temperatures weren't as high, and the nights were much colder. I had even seen frost on the ground on some mornings. Again, these were more signs that it was time to finish and get home to my family.

I walked to the lakeshore after the brief conversation ended. I wanted some time alone after spending much of the day around crowds of people. I was the only one on the shore, and having that beautiful lake all to myself was nice. The water was still. The smoke that had hung above the water earlier in the day was gone, and I had unobstructed views of the beauty surrounding me. I found a comfortable log at the water's edge, removed my shoes and socks, and immersed my feet in the cold water, relaxing and taking it all in. It was perfect.

Thinking about how my Pacific Crest Trail journey was coming to an end reminded me of the thoughts and feelings I'd had as I approached the end of my career in the air force. Just like the signs I'd received on the trail, signs had told me when it was my time to retire. "You'll know when it's time" is a common phrase in the military regarding the decision to retire, and it was true. I knew when it was my time.

I had planned on retiring as soon as I was eligible, right at the twenty-year point, but it wasn't time for me yet. My wife and I were still enjoying serving, and we still had much more we wanted to do and a lot more to contribute. We loved what we did and the people we got to serve with. Time, assignments, opportunities, great experiences, and connections with so many great people flew by, and before I knew it, I had served for thirty years. That is typically the maximum amount of time a chief master sergeant could serve before being required to retire. However, I was granted a waiver due to my position and was allowed to serve past that point, a rare opportunity that very few are given.

The positions I was selected for near the end of my career all came with the expectation of staying in place for minimum periods, typically two years. It took away some of the flexibility to retire exactly when I wanted to, but it also came with the benefits of knowing, far in advance, the exact date my assignment would be over, giving me time to plan and prepare.

My situation was slightly different from usual, though. I was allowed to serve in my final position for over three years, which meant retiring at the thirty-two-year point. However, my heart was set on fulfilling my childhood dream of hiking the PCT, and the date my waiver ended was outside the hiking season for the trail. The commander I was serving with knew how passionate I was about fulfilling my dream and supported my decision to retire early, allowing me to start my hike on the date I wanted.

Given my situation, the most important signs that it was time to retire came after it had already been approved and I'd selected the date for my ceremony. The first was thirty days before my ceremony, when I attended the promotion of a member of my organization pinning on the rank of chief master sergeant. The exact number changes yearly, but about 260,000 enlisted airmen are on active-duty service in the United States Air Force. Of that number, only 1 percent are authorized, by Congress, to serve in the rank of chief—about 2,600 airmen at the time.

Since my waiver had allowed me to serve beyond the time when most were required to retire, only one other active-duty chief in the entire air force had been serving longer than I had. I was literally almost the "old guy" and was at the promotion for one of the newest chiefs. Not only was his promotion ceremony a special event for him and his family, but it was also a special moment for me. I thought about my time as a chief and everything that had happened in the air force, our country, and the world during that period. I knew he would see and do incredible things during his time as a chief, just as I had.

I was excited for him. The look on his face as his new stripes were pinned on reminded me of how I felt when I was promoted to chief nearly ten years earlier. Along with the stripes came a realization of the significant responsibility to come. The new chief looked young, but I knew he was ready for what lay ahead. I had worked with him for the past two years. I saw how much he cared about his people and the lengths he went to take care of them. I saw how much the people around him admired and respected him too. He was the perfect example of what a chief should be and was the right leader, promoted at the right time, to do great things for the people he served.

After the ceremony, I shook his hand and congratulated him and his family. I held on to his hand a little longer than usual, knowing he was the last new chief I would congratulate while still in uniform. I also knew it was time for me to get out of the way so new chiefs like him could bring in fresh perspectives, shake things up, and continue to improve the air force in ways I no longer could.

The second sign occurred two weeks later. I was nearly ten miles into a training hike on the running trail that winds around the perimeter of Scott Air Force Base. The all-too-familiar sight of a white-and-blue air force C-40 (Boeing 737 modified for military use) came into my view. It taxied past me, about a hundred yards away, turned around at the end of the runway, and sat for a few moments as it prepared to take off. On that airplane were my commander and a team of senior leaders from our organization. They were headed to Europe to engage with service members in the region and with military leaders and dignitaries from a few of our allied nations.

**186** Jason France

I stopped and watched the plane take off, realizing that it was the first overseas trip I wouldn't be on with my commander since I arrived twenty-seven months ago. A commander and senior enlisted leader share a special bond that no other two leaders in a military organization have. It's a bond based on trust, openness, and honesty, a bond that transcends the ranks those two leaders hold. My bond with him was one of the closest of my career. The respect and admiration I had for him as an officer, leader, man, and friend made our connection even stronger. Watching that airplane take off felt strange. All I could think was *I should be on that plane.*

I stood motionless as I watched the plane disappear from my sight. I felt conflicted. *What am I doing here? I need to be there for my boss. I'm letting him down.*

Then reality set in. The plane still took off without me. *Everything will be fine without you there. The mission will continue. You're right where you need to be.* I continued my hike.

Even more meaningful were the important family events I was able to attend since I didn't go on that trip. The first was celebrating Joseph's sixteenth birthday, a huge milestone for any child and parent. I also picked him up from one of his track practices that week and shared in his excitement about breaking a personal record for his two-hundred-meter sprint time. His hard work, commitment to excellence, dedication to his team, and self-discipline inspired me and always made me want to work harder in all those areas. I was exactly where I needed to be that day.

Five days later we all celebrated my wife's birthday. She loves butterflies, and we surprised her with a trip to the Sophia M. Sachs Butterfly House in St. Louis. To see the smile on her face as we walked through the exhibits, surrounded by hundreds of beautiful butterflies, may have been more of a gift to me than it was for her. I couldn't take my eyes off her all day. Her smile and the way she looked at me were different. I don't know if it was because she was surrounded by such beauty or because we were so close to

Five Million Steps **187**

having more time to do things like we did that day. The reason didn't matter, though. I saw her beautiful smile and was exactly where I needed to be.

And finally, a few days after that, I was there when Justin brought home an award for earning straight A's in fifth grade, on top of the other awards he had received for his grades, being on the honor roll, and earning the Student of the Month award twice that year. We had moved five times since he was born because of my career, and he was attending his fourth school. That's the life of a military kid and one of the many challenges they face, all while not having a choice. He handled all our moves well, viewing them as opportunities, not burdens. He maintained a positive attitude, worked hard, and was rewarded for his efforts. I was exactly where I needed to be that day.

I had missed so many important events during my three decades of service, and I would have missed all those as well if I had been on that trip. Again, all signs that it was the right time for me to retire.

The final event occurred seven days before my retirement ceremony. I was honored to be the guest speaker at an Airman Leadership School graduation, the last air force event I would speak at before retiring, and the last where I would formally recognize the accomplishments of others while in uniform. Airman Leadership School is the foundational leadership course for enlisted airmen, and it's the first level of enlisted professional military education an airman can attend throughout their career. Graduation from the course is required before supervising other airmen and being promoted to staff sergeant, the first noncommissioned officer rank.

As part of the sequence of events for the graduation, the class leader, typically the senior student, addresses the class. Their address is given before the graduation speaker delivers their speech. I had attended countless graduation ceremonies throughout my career and was the guest speaker at many of them. That day the class leader gave one of the best speeches I've ever heard. Her words inspired everyone in the room. We could feel her excitement to lead and supervise young airmen after graduating. We were all moved by the pride and passion she displayed. She was years ahead of where I'd been at that point in my career. Her speech captured me so much that I nearly forgot it would soon be my turn to take the stage to give mine. And when I gave my speech, I was smiling from ear to ear the entire time, not because of what I was saying but because of what she had said. I never doubted the talent of the young airmen, but I walked away that day knowing the air force's future was in great hands. It was the last sign that it was the right time to retire.

•  •  •

A loud burst of laughter echoed from the lodge behind me, bringing me back to the PCT. Several more hikers had gathered on the patio as the day came to an end. Realizing it would be the last big gathering of hikers I would spend time with before finishing the trail, I left the lakeshore to join them. In the coming days, we would all leave Stehekin at different times. Some were staying there for a zero-day, some were waiting for other members of their trail family to catch up so they could finish at the same time, and one was waiting for his father, who had hiked the PCT years ago, to arrive on the ferry the following day so they could touch the terminus together. Some, like me, would finish our journeys alone. Not only were we leaving at different times, but our paces, the miles we would hike each day, and where we would camp each night would all be different.

It was one of the best times I had on the trail and certainly the most I'd laughed during my hike. We shared stories, most full of embellishments that had grown over time, making them far more entertaining than what had happened in reality. There were intimate details about embarrassing experiences we had or witnessed others having, many revolving around our use of "cat holes" or having "poop emergencies," both topics that were always good for laughs. The chafing of thighs, lower backs, nipples (not only me), and between the cheeks, and the remedies (pro tip: Vagisil for chaffing!) that we used to treat them. There were also the stories of extreme blisters, popping them—sometimes causing them to squirt far enough to hit other hikers—pulling off large patches of skin that remained after they were popped, taping all ten blistered toes, and dealing with nasty infections. Then came the stories of navigation errors: sometimes being lost for hours before finding the trail again, forgetting equipment in camp or at a break spot and rushing back, sometimes miles, to retrieve the forgotten items, and how we earned our trail names.

There were so many incredible stories about what we had experienced. They were stories only hikers could understand, appreciate, and be comfortable talking about. We were indeed a family, and it was nice to forget, for those few moments, that our journeys were coming to an end and we would no longer be surrounded by people who understood us the way we understood each other. I was ready to finish the trail, but I didn't want the experience to end. *Man, these people are amazing. I'm so going to miss this.*

The three days that followed flew by. I was more focused and aware of my surroundings than on any other section of the trail. I completely immersed myself in the experience, being present in every moment and hoping to remember every detail. I recorded no video footage and took only a few photos. I talked with everyone I passed on the trail, though, as I knew all along that the people I shared the adventure with were the best part of it all. The sounds, the views, the smells, the entire experience hit me differently in that stretch. I cherished every step and every minute, and before I knew it, I was setting up my last camp, only fourteen miles from the northern terminus and the end of my journey of a lifetime.

I had hiked over twenty-six miles that day and felt it was light work compared with my earliest days on the trail. I had hiked only eleven miles on my first day, and it was three weeks before I could hike over twenty miles in a day. I found a great camp spot and shared it with only a few other hikers.

**190** Jason France

It was quiet, calm, and peaceful, much different from the crowded, noisy camps I remembered from the first few hundred miles. Setting up camp was effortless; I was incredibly efficient from executing my camp routine over a hundred times in the past five months.

I enjoyed my dinner alone, watching the colors of the sky change as the sun set behind a ridge I was facing. Stunning yellows, oranges, and reds made the clouds above the ridge appear bright pink. I had known there would be a last camp on the trail for me, but I was surprised at how emotional I was when that night arrived. Thoughts of my experiences over the last five months raced through my mind as I lay in my tent, but I fell asleep quickly and had a good night's rest.

I woke up late for the last time on my final day. I had told myself countless nights that I'd get an early start the next day, but I rarely did. It was September 10, 2021. I had planned my finish date over a week before and put in extra miles each day to finish on the tenth, the day before the twentieth anniversary of the attacks on our nation on September 11, 2001. The events of 9/11 not only changed life as we knew it in our country, but that date was a significant turning point in my career and personal life. I didn't want to celebrate the end of my journey on Patriot Day. That day is sacred to me, and I felt I owed it to all who lost their lives to keep that day for them, and only them.

It was cold that morning, just above freezing, and it was hard for me to leave the warmth of my tent. But it was time for me to get moving, knock out those last fourteen miles, and begin the journey home. Despite breaking camp quickly to stay warm and get on the trail as soon as possible, the small details from those few minutes are still burned in my mind. The smell of my coffee, the steam from my pot, and its warmth in my freezing hands. Struggling to close that one tricky zipper on my tent that had been giving me trouble since before Tehachapi. Putting away the tent stake that I had bent near Crater Lake while setting up camp in the dark. And tapping out the tiny rocks and pieces of tree needles and bark from my shoes before putting them on the feet that had carried me thousands of miles—all for the last time before touching the terminus.

Once I got on the trail and warmed up, and once the excitement and endorphins kicked in, I was flying. At one point, I checked my watch and realized I had covered six and a half miles in under two hours, much faster than I usually moved through rugged terrain like that. I couldn't feel my pack's weight or any lingering ailments I usually felt. My movement seemed effortless.

I looked at my inReach. I was at mile 2,652.6, less than one mile to go. A few minutes later, I saw a straight line extending through the forest as far as I could see, about twenty-five yards wide, where all the trees had been cleared. It was the border of the United States and Canada. I rounded a few more curves of the trail and heard voices not too far away. One more turn on the trail, and there it was: the northern terminus.

I had thought about this moment for years but didn't know what my reaction would be once it became a reality. I hadn't planned anything either. I was going to roll with whatever happened. Still, many questions ran through my mind as I got closer. *What am I supposed to do now? Am I supposed to yell something at the top of my lungs? Am I supposed to run to the end? Should I be crying right now? Cartwheels? Moonwalk?* I thought I would get choked up when I saw the terminus, but I didn't. I was recording my reaction with my phone, and I had a huge smile on my face as I said, "Aw man. There it is. Whoof." My gaze was fixed on the monument as I took my final steps.

I touched the monument at the northern terminus of the Pacific Crest Trail at 11:57 a.m., 144 days after starting my journey. I was congratulated by a handful of hikers who had arrived before me and were sitting near the monument. It felt great to share the experience with them, but in all honesty, something was missing. I had just finished the most challenging thing I had ever done in my life, physically, mentally, and emotionally. I was proud of my accomplishment and excited to be finished, but strangely, part of me felt empty and alone. My family wasn't there with me to share the achievement.

I popped open the can of Pabst Blue Ribbon I'd bought in Skykomish, Washington, and carried for the last 188 miles. It was the best beer I've had in my life. And it was also the beer I had worked the hardest to earn.

Two more hikers, a couple who had completed the entire trail together, arrived as another hiker took the last few "photo finish" shots of me standing at the monument. I stepped away so they could have their moment just as I had. The rest of us clapped and cheered for them, and they celebrated with a long embrace and kiss. My heartache hit me again. *Man, I miss Monica and the boys. I wish they could be here with me.*

I sent them a message on my inReach. *We did it, guys! I'm done and will be on my way home soon. I love you!* My sons were still in school when I sent the message, but Monica responded quickly: *Congratulations, love. We're so proud of you. Love you!* Even though they couldn't be there with me, her text lifted my spirits and broke the funk I was in from missing them so badly.

I looked up from where I'd backed away from the monument. My new position allowed me to see it more clearly. Its construction was almost identical to the monument at the southern terminus, with five posts of different lengths arranged the same way and with similar inscriptions, but unlike the southern monument, the wood was dark, unpainted, much more weathered, and felt damp and cold to the touch. The words "strength" and "perseverance" came to mind as I stood there, admiring the monument.

Wedged between the two tallest posts were small American and Canadian flags. Taking a long look at the American flag on the monument was a special moment for me. That flag marked the end of the Pacific Crest Trail journey for me and countless other hikers. It reminded me of the American flag used during my retirement ceremony, marking the end of my air force career. It also reminded me of the most special moments I had on that day.

Five Million Steps **193**

My sons surprised me during the ceremony by coming up on stage to read statements they had each prepared. Joseph was first. "At a young age, when I heard the word 'hero,' I would instantly picture superheroes from the movies, such as The Flash, who was always my favorite. Although, over time, while growing up and gaining a better understanding of things happening around me, I think of someone else when hearing the word 'hero.' I instantly think of my dad, Jason France. . . . He raised my brother and me, teaching us that anything is possible, but he never left out the idea that we may struggle sometimes. He taught us to face our problems head-on and look at them as an opportunity to better ourselves."

Justin was next. "I just wanna say, Dad, that I'm very proud of you. You have served in the military for about thirty-one years! That's a lot of work. Most of that work you've done helped people's lives. And when I say you've helped, I mean you helped in a fantastic way. I also wanna say I love you. You have supported and helped me through my eleven years of life. I'm thankful for every second you're here with me."

There is no way to describe how meaningful their words were to me. It was my proudest moment as a father.

Monica stayed in her seat so our sons could have the time on the stage. She didn't have to say a word. We looked at each other for a few moments after Joseph and Justin finished and walked back to their seats. It was like we were the only two people in the room. The look in her eyes and the smile on her face told me everything. She had held our family together during all my time away. She was the one who'd always believed in me, even when I doubted myself. She was the one who'd endured my deployments, often alone. She gave me grace and showed patience and understanding when I returned, different each time than when I left. And she was the one who always picked me up when I was struggling. Now it was truly our time. There was no more putting the air force before our family. Our future was completely ours to build.

During my ceremony, many highlights of my career were mentioned: promotions; positions I'd held; decorations, medals, and awards I had received; the number of times I had deployed; and other seemingly important things, all tied to the word "success." But to me, those things didn't define my success at all. In my mind and heart, my success was sitting right in front of me: my wife and sons, my world.

They were what made me successful on my PCT journey too. They encouraged me to make my childhood dream a reality; they inspired me and gave me purpose to take on something this big; they lifted me on my most challenging days and supported me in every possible way. They were with me every step of my journey.

Now it was time for me to get home to them.

The final group of hikers, a large trail family who had been together for most of their hike, showed up. I loved seeing their excitement and feeling their energy. It was great to have one last celebration with some of the people I'd shared this experience with. Our entire group shared lunch and stories for an hour before we started trickling back down the trail toward Harts Pass. We were all so different but similar at the same time, and we had all just finished something incredible: hiking the Pacific Crest Trail.

CHAPTER 17

# AFTER THE TRAIL

My journey home started with a thirty-mile hike back to Harts Pass. In typical years, PCT hikers could enter Canada with a special permit that allows them to cross the border, continue on a nine-mile trail that brings them to Manning Park, British Columbia, and find their way home from there. Entry into Canada was prohibited due to COVID-19 restrictions, though, so we all had to turn around, retrace our steps back to Harts Pass, and find our way back to civilization from there.

I split my return to the pass into two days since I didn't leave the terminus until around 2:00 p.m. I was happy to have that time to begin absorbing what I had just experienced and start reflecting on what I'd gained before returning to the "real world." I knew I was a different person than when I took my first steps 144 days before, and I knew it would take months, and in some areas years, to realize all the ways the trail had changed me.

My initial thoughts were about how quickly my journey had flown by and how powerful the collection of moments was. I had experienced in under five months what would have taken me years to experience in daily life, and it seemed to pass in the blink of an eye. I have shared most of my reflections and experiences throughout this book, but starting my journey

**197**

home, retracing some of my steps on the trail, I found myself trying to capture and put into words what exactly it was that I'd gained from the experience as a whole. I knew the journey itself was the greatest reward, but I was expecting a big "aha" moment and felt disappointed when it didn't come. But then it did. *The answers will come with time. Don't rush it.* And I realized my hike back to Harts Pass gave me two more days on the trail. *Don't let these moments pass.* So I stopped overthinking it, brought my mind back to the trail, and simply enjoyed my last few miles to camp.

Wanting one final night of solitude, I found a small flat spot next to the trail near Woody Pass. Continuing the short distance to the same large campsite I had stayed at the previous night would have meant sharing it with the crowd of hikers that were a day behind me, preparing for their final push to the terminus. Another tent was already set up near the spot I chose, but far enough away to still give me the solitude I was looking for.

I hadn't seen anyone around the other tent, but as I was setting up mine, I heard what sounded like faint mumbling and movement inside the tent, just before there was a loud zipping noise and a hiker shot out. He looked familiar, but I wasn't sure if we had met before. I assumed he had set up in preparation for hiking to the terminus the next day.

"What's up, man? How's it going?" I shouted over to him.

He stood and looked down at his tent with a scowl. He didn't look over at me or say anything. He just shot one hand up into the air, briefly acknowledging me, before quickly pulling his hand back down.

*Well, all right. Looks like this dude is having a bad day.* "You hitting the terminus tomorrow?"

"Nah, man. I hit it this morning," he snapped, still not looking at me.

*I guess we missed each other on the trail today.* "Awesome! Congrats! How does it feel to be done?"

"It fucking sucks!" he snapped at me again, finally looking up.

Then I recognized him. It was Stilts. We had never spoken before, but

I had seen him a few times since crossing into Washington and heard from other hikers that he had hiked the Appalachian and Continental Divide Trails in previous years. Finishing the PCT meant he had earned his "triple crown," having hiked the three longest national scenic trails in the United States. *How could it suck to be the newest triple crowner?*

Confused, I asked him, "You okay, man? You're Stilts, right? Didn't you just get your triple crown?"

"Yeah, I did. But now what? I don't know what the hell I'm supposed to do."

"Whatever you want to, bro!"

"Yeah. Whatever. Hey, man, I'm not trying to be a dick or anything, but I'm really not in the mood to talk to anyone right now."

"Got it, bro. Sorry to bother you. Take care."

And that was that. I had no idea what had made him feel that way. I personally thought it was an amazing accomplishment. *To each his own, I guess.*

Heavy winds picked up as I finished setting up camp and was about to eat my dinner. I ended up eating inside my tent after tying down all the extra guy lines I hardly ever used, stacking rocks on top of the stakes, and bringing all my gear inside with me. It turned out to be the windiest night I experienced on the hike. It slammed my tent around all night, waking me over and over just as I fell asleep.

Stilts's comments kept coming back to me, and I couldn't get the thought of *Now what?* out of my head. *Maybe he has a point.* I had been so focused on the experience and trying to be present for myself during my hike that I hadn't thought much about what I would do after the trail. In fact, I'd intentionally avoided those thoughts when they arose. But lying there in my tent, I realized those thoughts were no longer avoidable.

The winds stopped just before daylight, and I got two hours of good sleep before getting back on the trail at eight o'clock for the twenty-mile hike to Harts Pass. Stilts was gone by the time I woke up.

The entire day, my last actual day on the PCT, was surreal. I was revisiting areas I had already passed on my journey north, but this time, heading south, I saw them from a completely different perspective. The spots were the same, still as beautiful as before, but the rush of excitement upon seeing them for the first time was gone. I had completed my goal of reaching the terminus. My mind was no longer focused on enjoying the trail and making my way to Canada. It was focused on getting home. It was the strangest feeling.

The day was filled with happy reunions and emotional farewells. I passed hikers I had shared my amazing experience with as they made their final push to the terminus. For most, it would be the last time we would ever see each other. Finally, arriving at Harts Pass just before 4:00 p.m., I finished my "bonus miles" on the PCT and officially started my journey home.

It was as if a switch flipped in my mind as soon as I stepped off the trail and onto the primitive dirt road that led eighteen miles to the small town of Mazama. My hike was over, and I just wanted to get home to my family. It would be three long days of waiting, but luck was on my side. Moments after stepping onto the road, I got a ride to Mazama from a couple who had just finished a day hike near the pass. We shared stories about our life adventures the whole way into town.

My luck continued when I got into town and found a spot at the local hostel. I had a hot shower, washed my clothes, and reunited and shared dinner with some of the group I had celebrated with at the terminus. The following morning, a couple from my hometown whom I've known since high school picked me up and brought me to Seattle, where I would fly home to St. Louis. They had followed my journey and encouraged me the whole way. Seeing them again after all those years was the perfect way to spend my final day in Washington before heading home to my family.

・・・

Two days later I was finally reunited with my family, and what an amazing feeling it was to have them back in my arms. Monica and Justin picked me up from the airport. I first saw them as I came down the escalator to the baggage claim area. Justin held a sign that said "Family Looking for Adventure Dude!"

As soon as he saw me, he ran up the stairs next to the escalator, leaned over the railing, and hugged me, holding on tightly as the escalator pulled me down. Monica greeted me at the bottom with a big hug, and seconds later we all shared a family embrace. I was reunited with Joseph later that night when he came home from work. "Adventure Dude" was finally home. My heart was happy. I was whole again.

The days that followed were filled with love, hugs, and laughter as we spent time reconnecting. All the little things I had missed were even more meaningful when I got home. Waking up next to Monica, feeling her warmth, not wanting to get out from under the sheets. Sharing our morning coffee, still with messy hair and sleepy eyes, a time when I find her so incredibly beautiful. The smiles on the boys' faces when they walk in the door from school, hearing their laughter echo throughout the house, and seeing their shoes lying next to the couch. And all of us sitting together for dinner or on the couch watching a movie. I loved every moment. They caught me up on everything I'd missed during my five months away, and I shared stories, photos, and videos of my adventures. I also reconnected with friends who supported me along the way, and I thanked them for all they had done for me.

Slowly, I became accustomed to the conveniences of life at home again. I realized on the trail that I had taken many of those things for granted: shelter, a bed, lights, air conditioning, easy access to any kind of food I desired, a refrigerator, a stove, a microwave, a coffee maker, internet, cellular

Five Million Steps **201**

service, a shower, a washer and dryer, a car—the list goes on.

One example that sticks out is what I had to do to get water on the trail. I often had more than ten miles between water sources—the longest stretch I remember was twenty-one. Most of my water was collected from sources in remote places: springs, creeks, or lakes. Many were directly on or close to the trail, and some were up to a mile away on a side trail. I had to check the map at each water source to find out where the next one was and determine how much water I would need to make it to the next source.

Once I figured that out, I had to collect the water in one of the bottles or a bag I was carrying, sometimes from a shallow, muddy creek or a spring pipe releasing only a tiny flow. Then I had to filter it, carefully separating the filtered water from the "dirty" and potentially contaminated water. I had to repeat that process to fill every container I carried, sometimes up to five one-liter bottles. If the water was flowing well from the source, this would only take a few minutes. If it was flowing slowly or was difficult to collect (think scooping from a mud puddle), it took much longer—at times thirty minutes to collect only one liter. Then I had to carry and ration it between sources. My largest water carry was six liters, weighing over thirteen pounds.

It was an art with quite a few variables, and it took a long time to perfect, but it was a necessary part of life on the trail. I learned to appreciate the process and the water itself much more, a convenience I admittedly took for granted before my hike. In contrast, our house now has seven sinks, two refrigerators with water and ice dispensers, and a water cooler with a stockpile of five-gallon bottles. At any moment, I am only a few steps away from as much fast-flowing clean water as I want.

Although I appreciated many of the conveniences I had missed while on the trail, things I didn't, such as the complexities of our world and everyday life, quickly crept back in. My five months on the trail had given me more of an escape than I initially realized. Many of the things I had disconnected from on the PCT hit me harder than they had before.

Throughout my life, I had conditioned myself to ignore, and in some cases just accept, things that became "normal" in our society. Seemingly everyone around me stuck to their screens, disconnected from the people and world around them. Social media has so much power and influence over people, causing us to constantly seek validation, believe distorted pictures of reality, and chase idealistic views of what life "should" look like. News outlets focus primarily on negativity, covering the bad while neglecting the good in the world, sensationalizing insignificant events, and fueling the growing divide in our nation with misinformation. Then there's the belief that everything in our lives must move fast. There's a desire for constant stimulation, that every moment should be filled with activity, words, or sound. And there's the need for instant gratification instead of appreciating the things that take time to create, earn, and achieve.

I started missing life on the trail more as time went on. I missed being surrounded by nature: the beautiful views, sounds, and smells, the richness of the experience. I missed watching the sunsets while sitting in camp, waking in the middle of the night to see a sky full of stars, and being awakened by the sun peeking over the horizon. I missed the euphoric feeling that came with the rush of endorphins that hit every day on the tough stretches of trail. I missed the clarity, sense of purpose, and feeling of accomplishment that came with a hike of that scale. The path was clear, linear, and simple, and I knew exactly what I had to do to reach my goal: just put one foot in front of the other. And I missed the community of people who had the same passion for the outdoors as I did. My connections with people I met on the trail were fading, and on top of that, so were the connections I'd made with people I'd served with in the military.

But as time passed, the things I gained on the PCT became clearer. I wouldn't let those experiences—the learning and growth—go to waste. With the end of my PCT journey and my career in the air force came incredible opportunity, freedom, and the choice to shape my future. It was time to ask the "Now what?" questions and turn those answers into reality.

It started with the small things. Too much negativity in the news? Turn it off. Don't like what I'm seeing on social media? Change what I'm looking at and who I'm connected with. Missing the trail? Get outside. Thinking about someone I haven't talked to in a while? Reach out to them. Progress on the small things led to progress on the bigger things.

The biggest "Now what?" question I had to answer was what my new career path would be. After spending over three decades in the air force, with a great deal of that time away from my family, my priority was being able to spend more time with them. I also needed a career that would fuel my passion for connecting with and helping people, giving me a sense of purpose and providing the fulfillment I enjoyed during my air force career. Those desires led me to become an executive coach, an adjunct professor, and a leadership development trainer. Each path has allowed me to share my experiences from my air force career and my PCT journey to help others grow.

My "Now what?" as a hiker was answered by maintaining connections with hikers I'd encountered and sharing my experiences to help others in the hiking community through online hiking forums, social media groups, and my YouTube channel. I returned to the trail again in 2022, hiking the five-hundred-mile Colorado Trail. It was a new, unknown adventure that allowed me to reconnect with myself and keep my passion for the outdoors alive. And there will be many more hiking adventures in my future.

But one of the biggest "Now what?" answers didn't come from me. It came from my family, friends, and connections I made throughout my military career and during my PCT hike. They gave me the inspiration, encouragement, and support I needed to start the next journey: writing this book. Thank you for joining me.

# ABOUT THE AUTHOR

Jason France is the founder and CEO of Elevate Leadership Solutions, providing executive coaching, professional development, and professional speaking services. He served in the United States Air Force for over thirty-one years, retiring as a command chief master sergeant and the command senior enlisted leader of the United States Transportation Command.

Jason was born and raised in Oak Harbor, Washington, where his passion for the outdoors began and continues today. He has hiked over 3,500 miles since retiring from the Air Force, completing three of America's national scenic trails: the Pacific Crest Trail, Colorado Trail, and Tahoe Rim Trail. Jason has many more adventures in his sights.